To Carl,
Mentor, and friend
with my gratitude

Joel

August 29, 2008

BOUNDLESS LOVE

The Parable of the Prodigal Son and Reconciliation

Joel W. Huffstetler

Foreword by Carl R. Holladay

D1248642

University Press of America,® Inc.
Lanham · Boulder · New York · Toronto · Plymouth, UK

Copyright © 2008 by
University Press of America,® Inc.
4501 Forbes Boulevard
Suite 200
Lanham, Maryland 20706
UPA Acquisitions Department (301) 459-3366

Estover Road
Plymouth PL6 7PY
United Kingdom

Library of Congress Control Number: 2008925822
ISBN-13: 978-0-7618-4091-6 (paperback : alk. paper)
ISBN-10: 0-7618-4091-5 (paperback : alk. paper)

The Scripture quotations contained herein are from the New Revised Standard
Version Bible, copyright ©1989 by the Division of Christian Education of the
National Council of Churches of Christ in the U.S.A., and are used by
permission. All rights reserved

♻™The paper used in this publication meets the minimum
requirements of American National Standard for Information
Sciences—Permanence of Paper for Printed Library Materials,
ANSI Z39.48—1984

To Fred and Dottie Williams,
With my love and gratitude

TABLE OF CONTENTS

Foreword

Among the teachings of Jesus recorded only in Luke's Gospel, none is more memorable—or powerful—than the story of the prodigal son. With vivid imagery, Luke depicts three sharply profiled, strong characters: the younger son, the father, and the older brother. Luke paints their portraits for us but we supply the details and associations. We quickly identify with each character. We can remember when we wandered far from home, or waited patiently for someone to come back, or felt resentment when we should have felt joy. Part of the story's magic is how it plays with the metaphor of home. At one level, the story is about leaving and returning home. But it also depicts journeys of the soul—spiritual pilgrimages—that occur within the tense interplay between alienation and reconciliation.

Several things commend Joel Huffstetler's exposition of this unforgettable Lukan parable. For one thing, he trusts the story to speak for itself. He points to the story by skillfully reporting the scholarly insights of others. And yet, he has read the story for himself and on his own terms. He, too, has gained insights from this powerful story, and he shares them generously with the readers. For another, his exposition reflects a teacher's instincts. Convinced that this story has much to say to contemporary readers, Joel offers guidance in how it can be read by the church. He reports textual complexities honestly, confident that mature readers will welcome such discussion.

Besides the rich exposition of the parable and the interpretive possibilities it holds for discerning readers, we also find hopeful proposals about reconciliation. Religious communities experiencing the alienating—and enervating—effects of division and alienation, are invited to probe this story once again for what it can teach us about achieving an equilibrium informed by love and humility rather than arrogance.

Carl R. Holladay
C. H. Candler Professor of New Testament
Emory University
Candler School of Theology
Atlanta, Georgia

Preface

This small book evolved from a Lenten series offered in 2007 at St. Luke's Episcopal Church, Cleveland, Tennessee. The series was titled, "Boundless Love: The Parable of the Prodigal Son," and offered an overview of the scholarship on Luke 15:11-32, as well as commentary on what scholars generally agree are the parable's key points. In researching the scholarship on the parable, I was struck by how relatively few monographs have been published on what is, arguably, Jesus' most familiar and most beloved teaching. When the Lenten series was finished, I kept reading and kept researching the scholarship on this extraordinary story, an ancient parable which is as fresh and as relevant today as it was when first told nearly 2,000 years ago. In considering what particular focus a small book on Luke 15:11-32 might take, I chose the subject of reconciliation. The need for reconciliation affects all persons in one way or another. For persons interested in biblically-based reconciliation, whatever the particulars of their situations, it is difficult to imagine a more instructive passage than the parable of the Prodigal Son. Though there are relatively few book-length treatments of Luke 15:11-32, the volume of scholarship on the parable in commentaries, the number of journal articles, and the countless references to the passage in spiritual and devotional books gives credence to the widely accepted view that these twenty-one verses of Luke's gospel are inexhaustible in meaning.

My only desire in offering the following reflections on the parable of the Prodigal Son is that readers might find this teaching of Jesus to be as challenging and as instructive as I continue to find it, particularly in regard to issues of reconciliation.

Joel W. Huffstetler
Cleveland, Tennessee
Epiphany 2008

Acknowledgments

A number of friends, family members, and colleagues have helped to make the publication of this book a reality and deserve special thanks. First, my heartfelt thanks to the members of St. Luke's Episcopal Church, Cleveland, Tennessee, who attended the Lenten series on Luke 15:11-32 in 2007. Your participation in the classes inspired me to keep reading and to pursue publishing a book on the parable. Thanks to Don Johnson, who early on in the project very graciously allowed me to borrow from his collection of books on Luke which far exceeds my own. Thanks to Dr. James Dunkly, whose class on Luke in the summer of 2007 at The School of Theology, Sewanee, inspired me to expand the scope of the original plan for the book and to keep working at it. Thanks to Dr. Carl Holladay for his very gracious contribution of a Foreword. Dr. Holladay's affirmation of the contents of my first book and his encouragement to pursue other writing projects played a very large part in my decision to write this book. Thanks to Brenda Martin, who somehow can decipher my atrocious handwriting, and who typed the first two drafts of this project (the second during the busiest time of the year) with her usual expertise and care. Thanks to Geneie Grant, the other half of the St. Luke's 'Dream Team', for her very important help with this project. Thanks to Brenda Hooper and Pam Boaz, who edited the second draft with their usual expertise and meticulous attention to detail, and who can attest to the fact that English was not by best subject! Thanks to Patti Williams and John Tallman, who proofread the final, camera-ready version of the project with great skill and care. Thanks to Samantha Kirk, my first contact at University Press of America, and to everyone there who have made this process such a pleasure. Thanks to Marylin Nicholls, who after my final Bible study at St. Andrew's Episcopal Church, Canton, North Carolina, in December, 1994, said: "I'm looking forward to reading your books." Well Marylin, sorry it took so long, but here you go.

Thanks to my parents, Joe and Pansy Huffstetler, who taught my sister and me a love and reverence for the Bible from our earliest days. I can remember those 'sword drills' at Ridgeview Baptist Church in Mount Holly, North Carolina, as if they had happened yesterday. My sister, Lee, was the writer in the family, and she brought far more vision, creativity, and skill to the task than I ever will. I do hope, however, that she would have liked this little book. Thanks to Debbie, who was vitally involved in this project at every stage, including typing the final, camera-ready draft, and who believes in me and my teaching ability far more than I. Her enthusiasm for and encouragement of this project mean more to me than words can adequately express. This book is dedicated to her parents, Fred and Dottie Williams, whose warm and gracious welcome into their family has been more wonderful than I could have hoped for or imagined.

Part I
Introduction

Then Jesus said,
"There was a man who had two sons.
The younger of them said to his father,
'Father, give me the share of the property that will belong to me.'
So he divided his property between them.
A few days later the younger son gathered all he had
and traveled to a distant country,
and there he squandered his property in dissolute living.
When he had spent everything, a severe famine took place
throughout that country, and he began to be in need.
So he went and hired himself out to one of the citizens of that country,
who sent him to his fields to feed the pigs.
He would gladly have filled himself with the pods that the pigs were eating;
and no one gave him anything.
But when he came to himself he said,
'How many of my father's hired hands have bread enough and to spare,
but here I am dying of hunger!
I will get up and go to my father, and I will say to him,
"Father, I have sinned against heaven and before you;
I am no longer worthy to be called your son;
treat me like one of your hired hands." '
So he set off and went to his father.
But while he was still far off, his father saw him and was
filled with compassion;
he ran and put his arms around him and kissed him.
Then the son said to him, 'Father, I have sinned against heaven
and before you; I am no longer worthy to be called your son.'
But the father said to his slaves,
'Quickly, bring out a robe—the best one—and put it on him;
put a ring on his finger and sandals on his feet.
And get the fatted calf and kill it,
and let us eat and celebrate;
for this son of mine was dead and is alive again;
he was lost and is found!'
And they began to celebrate.
Now his elder son was in the field;
and when he came and approached the house, he heard music and dancing.

> *He called one of the slaves and asked what was going on.*
> *He replied, 'Your brother has come, and your father has killed the fatted calf,*
> *because he has got him back safe and sound.'*
> *Then he became angry and refused to go in.*
> *His father came out and began to plead with him.*
> *But he answered his father,*
> *'Listen! For all these years I have been working like a slave for you,*
> *and I have never disobeyed your command;*
> *yet you have never given me even a young goat*
> *so that I might celebrate with my friends.*
> *But when this son of yours came back,*
> *who has devoured your property with prostitutes,*
> *you killed the fatted calf for him!'*
> *Then the father said to him,*
> *'Son, you are always with me, and all that is mine is yours.*
> *But we had to celebrate and rejoice,*
> *because this brother of yours was dead and has come to life;*
> *he was lost and has been found.'"*
>
> *Luke 15:11-32*

A prodigal child. A loving parent. A resentful sibling. A story involving arrogance, self-righteousness, repentance, compassion, and forgiveness; a story as relevant and as believable now as when it was first told some 2,000 years ago. In a mere twenty-one verses of Luke's gospel, we encounter the profoundly instructive parable of the Prodigal Son, Luke 15:11-32. This earthy story presents a picture of family life to which the vast majority of readers can relate. The ongoing relevance and applicability of Luke 15:11-32 comes from the reality that most readers, when honest with themselves, have no trouble finding themselves in the parable. The story of the prodigal, his older brother, and their father transcends boundaries of culture, ethnicity, and language. It is timeless and seemingly inexhaustible in meaning.

In evaluating the parable, Henri Nouwen writes: "All of the Gospel is there." [1] All of the gospel found in a mere twenty-one verses—an extraordinary claim. Nouwen goes on to say: "More than any other story in the Gospel, the parable of the prodigal son expresses the boundlessness of God's compassionate love." [2] Through its vivid, believable portrayal of God's amazing love, Nouwen claims that the parable of the Prodigal Son, "...encapsulates the core message of the Gospel." [3]

One can argue that the core message of the gospel is, indeed, reconciliation. The essence of the gospel message is the offer to human beings of reconciliation with God through the grace of Jesus, the Christ. And in the love of Jesus, Christian sisters and brothers are reconciled to one another and empowered to serve the world in his name. The offer of the gospel, the good news, is union with God, and with one's sisters and brothers, in Jesus. In a word—reconciliation.

This book is a reflection on Luke 15:11-32, with a specific focus on reconciliation. In our time, many Christians find themselves increasingly divided over a variety of ethical issues, and, at a deeper, more foundational level, over issues of biblical interpretation and authority. Discussions within Christian circles oftentimes are characterized by harshness and judgmentalism rather than forebearance, or mutual respect. In some circles there is talk of schism, of 'irreconcilable differences'. The argument of the text which follows is that the parable of the Prodigal Son has much to teach the Christian Church at this time in its history when there is so much talk and experience of division within the 'family'. The contention of these pages is that Nouwen is correct; the core message of the gospel can be found in Luke 15:11-32.

Robert Brown, among many other interpreters, asserts that the parable of the Prodigal Son can, "...scarcely be overvalued." [4] John R. Donahue makes the claim, echoed by other scholars, that: "No section of the New Testament has received as much attention and extravagant praise as this parable."[5] So compelling is the parable that: "Its drama has enchanted believer and non-believer."[6] Indeed, it is true that among those who have only a cursory knowledge of the New Testament's contents, the parable of the Prodigal Son is likely familiar, at least in broad outline.

Richard C. Trench holds that Luke 15:11-32 is, "...the pearl and crown of all the parables of Scripture..."[7] R. C. H. Lenski agrees that this parable is indeed the "crown" of all parables, having, "...no equals in all literature." [8] A. M. Hunter claims that the Prodigal Son is, by common consent, "...the paragon of all parables." [9]

Luke 15:11-32 is so compelling, and its relevance so enduring, in part because it consists of such understandable and believable characters. Along these lines, Burton Scott Easton observes that this "perfect story" is told with "perfect simplicity." [10] Lenski says succinctly: "So brief the parable, but so stirring in every part." [11] Arland J. Hultgren refers to the parable as, "great art."[12] William Barclay sums up the thoughts of countless readers down through the years in stating: "Not without reason this has been called the greatest short story in the world."[13]

Kenneth Bailey claims that Luke 15:11-32 is a "matchless story." [14] In his view this parable is the, "...story of stories!"[15] Fred Craddock holds that the parable is "extraordinary" in its composition.[16] Hunter notes that Robert Bridges, the English poet (1844-1930), pronounced the parable to be, "...an absolutely flawless piece of work." [17] J. R. H. Moorman agrees that from the point of view of literary skill the parable is a "masterpiece."[18] Luke Timothy Johnson observes that this story is detailed enough to be referred to as an, "...extended parable, virtually a novella."[19]

Many New Testament scholars would agree, in their own words, with Nouwen's contention that the core message of the gospel is found in Luke 15:11-32. Norval Geldenhuys argues: "This parable deserves to be called the 'Gospel within the Gospel' because in it so many Gospel truths are proclaimed in such a beautiful and graphic manner."[20] Stephen C. Barton writes: "As a parable of divine grace and forgiveness, what Luke gives us here is unsurpassed." [21] Joachim Jeremias, one of the previous century's greatest interpreters of the parables, states: "The parable describes with the most impressive simplicity what God is like—his goodness, his grace, his great mercy, his abounding love." [22]

Regarding the parable's message of God's love and grace, J. Ellsworth Kalas claims: "No story could say it more beautifully or persuasively than this one." [23] In his view, hardly any story in the Bible is more effective in proclaiming God's love for the human race. He writes: "John 3:16 proclaims that God so loved the world that God gave the Son for our salvation, but this parable dramatizes that verse by showing the extremes of the reach of God's love." [24]

Regarding the parable's various usages and its lasting influence, Joseph Fitzmyer argues that the Prodigal Son has, more than any other gospel pericope, "...entered into varied discussions and presentations of human conduct." [25] James L. Price goes so far as to say: "Surely no part of Scripture is more widely known." [26] Among the parables of Jesus, Craddock claims that Luke 15:11-32 is "easily" the most familiar. [27] George B. Caird agrees that the Prodigal Son is the best known and best loved of the parables in the New Testament. This story, in Caird's view, is, "...justly treasured for its exquisite literary grace and penetrating delineation of character as well as for its assurance of a divine mercy surpassing all expectation." [28] Moorman concurs that this passage is "undoubtedly" the most loved of the parables, conveying, "...the depth of God's love for his erring children and the assurance of forgiveness and rehabilitation for all those who having sinned, have returned in penitence to the throne of grace." [29]

Without question, a large part of the reason this story is so universally loved is its earthiness, its believability. David L. Tiede notes: "This is a human story. Its power and appeal arise from the reality of its characters. None of them is a plaster saint." [30] In the words of Walter R. Bowie: "Here is not only an illustration applicable to human life. Here is life itself in its unmistakable reality." [31] While Luke 15:11-32 is, on the surface, simple and straightforward, it is, upon further consideration, extraordinarily rich in layers of meaning. Upon considered reflection, the parable is seemingly inexhaustible in meaning, depending upon the various points of view from which it can be studied. I. Howard Marshall observes: "Of all the parables this one is perhaps the easiest to interpret in broad outline and yet the most open to a variety of interpretation, dependent on where the main emphasis is thought to lie." [32] Price sagely notes: "Apparently its message cannot be captured once for all in summary, its meaning in popular paraphrase. Like an exquisite diamond, flashes of light and color are seen when it is examined closely." [33] Judith Lieu agrees, noting that the profound influence the parable has had on literary and artistic imagination demonstrates how difficult it is to limit its interpretation to a single message. [34]

From a textual standpoint, there are remarkably few issues with Luke 15:11-32. Except for a handful of attempts to demonstrate that the original parable consisted of verses 11-24, and that verses 25-32 were a later addition, nearly all New Testament specialists accept the parable's unity and authenticity. The parable, unique to Luke's gospel, fits well within his overall theme of God's love for 'sinners', for those persons currently outside of a loving relationship with God, and with the community of faith. It also addresses another of Luke's key themes—joy. John Drury notes that in Luke 15:11-32 these two widely recognized Lukan themes come together. The parable speaks to yet another of Luke's themes—repentance, a change or turning of mind and heart which Jesus longs to see in those currently outside of experiencing God's loving embrace. [35] Drury notes that like the parable of the Good Samaritan (Luke 10:29-37), the story in 15:11-32 exhibits many of Luke's trade-marks, "...a secular story without religious trappings, the well-to-do setting (people of property, with servants), journeying, [and] the moment when dereliction turns to comfort..." [36]

The immediate context of the parable, Luke chapter 15, focuses explicitly on the theme of the 'lost' becoming 'found'. Luke 15:1 makes it clear that "tax collectors" and "sinners" are approaching Jesus to listen to his teaching. The tax collectors and sinners represent the 'lost', those persons considered outside the boundaries of the life of the local synagogue. To the most zealous members of such local faith communities, the scribes and Pharisees, the tax collectors and sinners represent the 'wrong' kind of people, and they are critical of Jesus' willingness to be with them (15:2). In 15:3-32, Luke portrays Jesus' response to this criticism. Verses 3-10 contain the parable of the Lost Sheep. The one 'lost' sheep vis-à-vis the ninety-nine other 'found' sheep represents a repentant sinner. The lost sheep's being found is cause for rejoicing (15:6-7).

Verses 8-10 of chapter 15 present the parable of the Lost Coin. The woman's finding her one 'lost' coin after diligently searching for it is, again, cause for rejoicing (15:9). Jesus teaches that even the angels rejoice over one sinner's repentance (15:10).

In the parable of the Prodigal Son, it is no longer a sheep, nor a coin, but a child, a human being, who repents and is 'found'. Certainly the return of the prodigal son is cause for rejoicing (15:22-24, 32). In Luke 15, Jesus uses these three parables to counter his critics' condemnation of his association with tax collectors and sinners. It is the will of God for the 'lost' to be 'found', and such moments of reconciliation are to be greeted with joy. In the words of Robert C. Tannehill regarding the three parables of Luke 15: "In presenting God and Jesus as searchers for sinners, they also require the Lukan audience to show a similar concern and to rejoice when the lost return to God's people." [37]

The parable of the Prodigal Son is linked thematically with other passages in Luke emphasizing God's mercy, and passages warning against an arrogant, uncompassionate self-righteousness. In Luke 6:36, Jesus issues a call for his hearers to mirror in their own lives God's mercy. Verses 27-42 go on to warn against judgmentalism and self-righteousness.

Luke 10:29-37, the parable of the Good Samaritan, is, in effect, a 'sister' parable to the parable of the Prodigal Son. In 10:29-37, we encounter the issues of mercy, as well as a callous disregard of the person in need. Regarding the Samaritan's acts of compassion and mercy toward the helpless traveler, Jesus instructs his hearers to go and do likewise.

Similarly to Luke 15, in 11:37-54 the Pharisees and scribes are challenged to rethink their mindset which is opposed to Jesus' more merciful, compassionate outlook. Luke 14:7-14 contains more teaching urging Jesus' hearers away from self-righteousness and toward an orientation to compassion and mercy.

Following the parable of the Prodigal Son, in Luke 16:14-15 the Pharisees again come into criticism regarding their self-righteousness and are taught that, their contentedness notwithstanding, God knows their hearts (16:15). Also, in 18:9-14, the parable of the Pharisee and the Tax Collector, once again Luke portrays Jesus teaching that the tax collector's honesty and humility is a more healthy mindset than the Pharisee's presumptuous self-righteousness.

What follows is a study of Luke 15:11-32, with an emphasis on the parable's teaching regarding reconciliation. The first four chapters offer an overview of the scholarship on the parable's three main characters—the prodigal son, the compassionate father, and the resentful older brother, and of the parable's meaning in broad outline. Chapters 5-7 examine each of the main characters from the standpoint of reconciliation, studying what each of them has to teach readers regarding reconciliation in its various manifestations—with God, with fellow human beings, and, particularly, within the Christian Church itself. The Conclusion will offer summary comments on the parable of the Prodigal Son and its potential to inform, to guide, and to inspire followers of the Prince of Peace to choose reconciliation rather than division. The claim of this book is that Luke 15:11-32 is indeed a matchless story, the story of stories, which portrays in a most compelling way God's boundless compassion and love, the compassion and love followers of Jesus are to embrace and to share. To quote Emil Brunner's summary statement regarding the parable: "Were we really to grasp it with all our heart, our life would overflow with joy and love." [38]

Notes

1.   Henri J. M. Nouwen, *The Return of the Prodigal Son: A Story of Homecoming* (New York: Doubleday, 1992), 15.
2.   Ibid., 36.
3.   Ibid., 64.
4.   Robert R. Brown, *Alive Again* (New York: Morehouse-Barlow, 1964), 8.
5.   John R. Donahue, *The Gospel in Parable: Metaphor, Narrative, and Theology in the Synoptic Gospels* (Philadelphia: Fortress Press, 1988), 151.
6.   Ibid.
7.   Richard C. Trench, *Notes on the Parables of Our Lord* (Westwood, NJ: Fleming H. Revell Company, 1953), 389.
8.   R. C. H. Lenski, *Commentary on the New Testament: The Interpretation of St. Luke's Gospel*. Hendrickson Publishers, Inc., edition. Second Printing (Peabody, MA: Hendrickson Publishers, 2001), 807.

9. Archibald M. Hunter, *Interpreting the Parables* (Philadelphia: Westminster Press, 1960), 60.

10. Burton Scott Easton, *The Gospel According to St. Luke: A Critical and Exegetical Commentary* (New York: Charles Scribner's Sons, 1926), 236.

11. Lenski, 807.

12. Arland J. Hultgren, *The Parables of Jesus: A Commentary*. The Bible In Its World. David Noel Freeman, General Editor (Grand Rapids: William B. Eerdmans Company, 2000), 82.

13. William Barclay, *The Gospel of Luke*. The New Daily Bible Study Guide (Louisville: Westminster John Knox Press, 1975), 242.

14. Kenneth E. Bailey, *The Cross and the Prodigal: Luke 15 Through the Eyes of Middle Eastern Peasants*. Second Edition (Downers Grove, IL: InterVarsity Press, 2005), 67.

15. Ibid., 87.

16. Fred B. Craddock, *Luke. Interpretation: A Biblical Commentary for Teaching and Preaching* (Louisville: John Knox Press, 1990), 186.

17. Hunter, 61.

18. John R. H. Moorman, *The Path to Glory: Studies in the Gospel According to St. Luke* (London: SPCK and Seabury Press, 1960), 187.

19. Luke Timothy Johnson, *The Gospel of Luke*. Sacra Pagina Series, Volume 3 (Collegeville, MN: The Liturgical Press, 1991), 236.

20. Norval Geldenhuys, *Commentary on The Gospel of Luke*. The New International Commentary on the New Testament (Grand Rapids: William B. Eerdmans Publishing Company, 1952), 406.

21. Stephen C. Barton, "Parables on God's Love and Forgiveness (Luke 15:11-32)." In *The Challenge of Jesus' Parables*. McMaster New Testament Studies. Richard N. Longenecker, Editor (Grand Rapids: William B. Eerdmans Publishing Company, 2000), 212.

22. Joachim Jeremias, *Rediscovering The Parables* (New York: Charles Scribner's Sons, 1966), 103.

23. J. Ellsworth Kalas, *The Parables of Jesus* (Nashville: Abingdon Press, 1997), 29.

24. Ibid., 37.

25. Joseph A. Fitzmyer, *The Gospel According to Luke X-XXIV*. The Anchor Bible (New York: Doubleday, 1995), 1083.

26. James L. Price, "Luke 15:11-32." *Interpretation* 31 (January, 1977): 64.

27. Craddock, *Luke*, 186.

28. George B. Caird, *The Gospel of Luke*. The Pelican Gospel Commentaries (Baltimore: Penguin Books, 1963), 182.

29. Moorman, 186.

30. David L. Tiede, *Luke*. Augsburg Commentary on the New Testament (Minneapolis: Augsburg Publishing House, 1988), 277.

31. Walter R. Bowie, *The Compassionate Christ: Reflections from the Gospel of Luke* (Nashville: Abingdon Press, 1965), 207.

32. I. Howard Marshall, *The Gospel of Luke: A Commentary on the Greek Text*. The New International Greek Testament Commentary (Grand Rapids: Paternoster Press, 1978), 604.

33. Price, 64.

34. Judith Lieu, *The Gospel of Luke*. Epworth Commentaries. Ivor H. Jones, General Editor (Peterborough: Epworth Press, 1997), 156.

35. John Drury, *The Gospel of Luke: A Commentary on The New Testament in Modern English*. The J. B. Phillips' Commentaries (New York: Macmillan Publishing Co., Inc., 1973), 155.
36. Ibid., 156.
37. Robert C. Tannehill, *Luke*. Abingdon New Testament Commentaries (Nashville: Abingdon Press, 1996), 239.
38. Emil Brunner, *Sowing and Reaping: The Parables of Jesus*. Tr. Thomas Wieser (Richmond: John Knox Press, 1946), 39.

Chapter One
The Prodigal Son

Then Jesus said,
"There was a man who had two sons.
The younger of them said to his father,
'Father, give me the share of the property that will belong to me.'
So he divided his property between them.
A few days later the younger son gathered all he had
and traveled to a distant country,
and there he squandered his property in dissolute living.
When he had spent everything, a severe famine took place
throughout that country, and he began to be in need.
So he went and hired himself out to one of the citizens of that country,
who sent him to his fields to feed the pigs.
He would gladly have filled himself with the pods that the pigs were eating;
and no one gave him anything.
But when he came to himself he said,
'How many of my father's hired hands have bread enough and to spare,
but here I am dying of hunger!
I will get up and go to my father, and I will say to him,
"Father, I have sinned against heaven and before you;
I am no longer worthy to be called your son;
treat me like one of your hired hands." '
So he set off and went to his father.

Luke 15:11-20a

In Luke 15:11-20a, the reader encounters one of the most familiar characters in all of scripture, indeed, in all of literature, the prodigal son. As was noted in the Introduction, persons with only a cursory knowledge of the New Testament are likely to be at least somewhat familiar with this presumptuous young man who breaks with the norms of the culture in which the story is cast. The prodigal's wish to receive his share of the inheritance and leave his family is the deepest insult possible to his father, and, ultimately, to his entire family.

In commenting on verse 12, Barclay observes, "...there is a certain heartless callousness in the request of the younger son."[1] Lenski notes that the radical nature of the request indicates: "His *heart* was no longer with his father."[2] Joel Green speaks for the vast majority of interpreters of the parable when he states that the son's request is, "...strikingly presumptuous."[3] John Nolland addresses the seriousness of the son's request when he asserts: "There is no doubt that the younger son is initiating a breakdown of the solidarity of the family..."[4]

Brunner frames the issue of the son's request for subsequent interpretation when he remarks, "...such egotism, stirs in the heart of each of us, and it is the root of all sin."[5] Commenting on the son's self-centeredness exhibited in his request in verse 12, Trench states: "Contemplated spiritually this request is the expression of man's desire to be independent of God, to become a god to himself (Gen. 3:5), and to lay out his life at his own will and for his own pleasure."[6] Nouwen observes that once the prodigal has expressed his wish to separate himself from his family, he has, "...embarked on the road to death."[7]

Over the years, commentators have wrestled at great length with whether the son's request to inherit his share of the estate early would have been legal in the society in which the story is cast. Most commentators agree that although such a request would have been highly unusual, and deeply insulting to the family, it would have been permissible in a legal sense. Bailey summarizes the scholarly consensus on this question succinctly: "The son has not broken the law. Rather he has broken his father's heart."[8] Regarding inheritance traditions in Jewish families in the cultural milieu in which the parable is set, relevant Old Testament passages include Numbers 27:8-11, 36:7-9; and Deuteronomy 21:15-17.

It is in verse 13 where we encounter the word from which Luke 15:11-32 receives its most common name. In verse 13, the reader learns that the son squandered his inheritance in dissolute living. The Greek word in play is *asōtōs*, typically rendered in English as "dissolute," "loose," or "riotous" behavior. The word occurs elsewhere in the New Testament in Ephesians 5:18; Titus 1:6; and I Peter 4:13. A relevant Old Testament passage is Proverbs 28:7, which pictures a prodigal son, a companion of gluttons, who shames his father.

Having squandered his inheritance in dissolute living, the prodigal son then finds himself in the midst of a famine-stricken environment. He becomes desperate enough to take employment feeding swine, the meanest state imaginable for a Jewish male from a prominent, indeed, from all appearances in the parable, a wealthy family. Passages relevant to Jewish customs regarding the uncleanness of swine include Leviticus 11:7; Deuteronomy 14:8; Isaiah 65:4; I Maccabees 1:47; II Maccabees 6:18, and 7:1. Verse 16 indicates that the prodigal would gladly have eaten the pigs' food, so desperate was his plight as, being in a foreign country, no one came to his aid. Ruth Etchells summarizes well the picture painted in verses 14-16: "It is an image, particularly in Jewish terms, of total abjectness."[9]

Among many interpreters, verse 17 is judged to be the key moment in the parable. Lenski puts it thusly: "The heart of the parable is stated in this sentence:

'He came to himself.' "[10] Bowie refers to, "...that unforgettable and searching phrase, 'When he came to himself.' "[11] Nouwen asserts that when the prodigal 'came to himself': "It was the rediscovery of his deepest self."[12] Brown shares Nouwen's terminology, and notes the parable's challenge to its readers to, "...rediscover our souls."[13] Trench agrees that the phrase, "he came to himself," conveys, "...words of deepest significance, from which we conclude that to come to one's self, and to come to God, are one and the same thing."[14]

A small minority of scholars doubt whether "he came to himself" marks genuine repentance on the part of the prodigal, suggesting instead that the desperation of his circumstances may account for a calculated decision to return home. The vast majority of scholars, however, see in verse 17 a genuine repentance, a turning around, a change of heart. Jeremias asserts that both the Hebrew and Aramaic background to the Greek rendered, "he came to himself," connote a genuine expression of repentance.[15] In further comments on 15:17, Jeremias states: "Repentance means learning to say 'Abba' again, putting one's whole trust in the heavenly Father, returning to the Father's house and the Father's arms."[16] Alfred Plummer agrees that the portrait in verse 17 is one of a repentant, humbled son, "longing" for home.[17] Brown concludes regarding verse 17 that, being repentant, the prodigal's dearest desire is to return home, "...to an environment with a heart."[18]

In verses 18-20a, the young son commits himself to arise (*anastàs*) and return to his father, willing to forfeit his status as a son and accept the lower status of a hired servant. The word "arise" occurs both in verses 18 and 20a. Stephen C. Barton suggests that, "...the repeated use of the participle *anastàs*, 'rising', in vv. 18 and 20 is suggestive of coming back to life—that is, resurrection."[19]

Verses 18-20a make clear that the prodigal is a changed man. There are no traces left of his arrogance, his egotism. He is humbled. As Barton suggests, his decision to arise and return home to his father is the beginning of a new life for him.

Luke 15:11-20a portrays one of the great reversals in all of literature. The prodigal's journey is one of moving from a life of security and prosperity to one of complete and utter despair. He has moved from being a member of a secure family to a life where he is starkly alone. From a picture of arrogance and presumptuousness in verse 12, verses 17-20 reveal a different young man, a changed person, who, having come to himself, summons the courage to return to his father.

Notes

1.   Barclay, *The Gospel of Luke,* 242.
2.   Lenski, 808.

3.   Joel B. Green, *The Gospel of Luke* (Grand Rapids: William B. Eerdmans Publishing Company, 1997), 580.
4.   John Nolland, *Word Biblical Commentary: Luke 9:21-18:34.* Volume 35B (Waco, TX: Word Incorporated, 1993), 782.
5.   Brunner, 37.
6.   Trench, 393.
7.   Nouwen, 48.
8.   Bailey, 42.
9.   Ruth Etchells, *A Reading of the Parables of Jesus* (London: Darton, Longman and Todd, Ltd.,), 30.
10.   Lenski, 812.
11.   Bowie, 208.
12.   Nouwen, 48.
13.   Brown, 52.
14.   Trench, 403.
15.   Jeremias, *Rediscovering the Parables*, 102.
16.   Ibid., 156.
17.   Alfred Plummer, *A Critical and Exegetical Commentary On The Gospel According to St. Luke.* The International Critical Commentary. Fifth Edition (Edinburgh: T & T Clark, 1896), 374.
18.   Brown, 85.
19.   Barton, 211.

Chapter Two
The Compassionate Father

But while he was still far off, his father saw him and was
filled with compassion;
he ran and put his arms around him and kissed him.
Then the son said to him, 'Father, I have sinned against heaven
and before you; I am no longer worthy to be called your son.'
But the father said to his slaves,
'Quickly, bring out a robe—the best one—and put it on him;
put a ring on his finger and sandals on his feet.
And get the fatted calf and kill it,
and let us eat and celebrate;
for this son of mine was dead and is alive again;
he was lost and is found!'
And they began to celebrate.

Luke 15:20b-24

Without question, the most commonly used title for Luke 15:11-32 is the parable of the Prodigal Son. Over the years, however, commentators have argued that the parable of the Prodigal Son is, in fact, misnamed, suggesting instead that titles such as the parable of the Loving Father, the parable of the Compassionate Father, the parable of the Forgiving Father, or the parable of the Waiting Father would be more appropriate regarding the essence of the story. Such is the power of the image of the father in Luke 15:11-32. It is, indeed, an unforgettable image, a compelling picture of love, compassion, forgiveness and acceptance which human beings long for but seldom experience in this life. In reflecting further on the portrayal of the father in the parable, one realizes that he is the personification of grace.

In his treatment of the parable, Craddock claims: "This is not a parable of a younger son and a parable of an older son, but a parable of a father."[1] Hultgren agrees, arguing that there can be little doubt that the father is the main character of the story, as it is his relationship with his two sons that is the, "...dynamic thread running throughout the parable."[2] In the words of Donahue, "...it is chiefly the father who gives shape to the drama."[3]

Many interpreters of Luke 15:11-32 maintain that the image of the father in the parable is the most compelling image of God in all of scripture. Among such interpreters is R. Alan Culpepper, who asserts: "No other image has come closer to describing the character of God than the waiting father..."[4] Wilfrid Harrington observes that the portrayal of divine love in the parable is "inconceivable" to human beings who struggle to grasp the depth of God's unconditional love for humanity.[5] Bailey goes so far as to claim that the "matchless" picture of the father in the parable, "...alone should shape our image of God as our heavenly Father."[6] John Drury comments: "The father is the original good parent..."[7]

Regarding the portrayal of the father in Luke 15:11-32, Herman Hendrickx cautions that, while his image is, unquestionably, lofty, his behavior must nonetheless represent a real human possibility. While no human being could possibly mirror the father's stunning love perfectly or without fail, it is nonetheless the pattern Christians are to follow: "Otherwise, one could attribute such forgiveness to God, who is different anyway, while at the same time considering it impossible or not required in the community."[8]

The father's predisposition to love and compassion, offered equally to both sons is, without question, a foundational understanding readers are to take from the parable. The father models the orientation that the followers of Jesus are to have toward their fellow human beings. Hultgren notes: "The attitude of the father toward his sons is not determined by their character, but his."[9] His character, as the parable will make clear as it unfolds, is grounded in compassion rather than judgment; he desires unity among loved ones, not estrangement.

Verse 20 makes clear that the father's first reaction to the vision of his young son's returning home is compassion. For all that has transpired, the father's response to the prodigal is grounded in mercy. The father does not wait patiently for the son to come to him but instead runs to meet him. Bailey suggests that a part of the father's compassion toward his son includes the father's concern for the villagers' reaction to the disgraced child. In Bailey's view, the father, "...takes upon himself the shame and humiliation due the prodigal."[10] Eduard Schweizer notes, from a cultural perspective, that in the Near East a mature man loses all his dignity when he runs.[11] N. T. Wright agrees that, given the culture in which the story is set, the father's racing to meet his son is significant, noting, "...senior members of families never do anything so undignified at the best of times, let alone in order to greet someone who should have remained in self-imposed ignominy."[12] Sirach 19:30 includes a reference to the cultural expectation of a mature man's dignified walk.

One can read the text of verse 20 to imply that the father was, indeed, looking for his son to return, actively hoping that at any moment the deeply loved and sorely missed child might return home. This plausible reading of verse 20b is reminiscent of Tobit 11:5-6, where Anna is portrayed as actively looking for the return of Tobias.

The latter part of 20b shows the father embracing and kissing his son. These are clear signs of reconciliation offered by the father. The son is truly welcomed home, unconditionally. This scene of reconciliation recalls Genesis 33:4, where Esau runs to meet his estranged brother Jacob. Esau takes the initiative to embrace Jacob and to kiss him in an unambiguous gesture of love and acceptance. Trench points out that a kiss such as the one offered by the father to the prodigal is more than a mere token of affection, being *the* significant, and in the Near East well understood, pledge of reconciliation.[13] In addition to Genesis 33:4, the kiss offered to Absalom by David in II Samuel 14:33 provides further scriptural precedent for the scene portrayed in Luke 15:20b.

Importantly, Plummer notes that at this point in the narrative the young son has said nothing. The father, on first seeing and greeting the son so lovingly and warmly, does not yet know in what spirit he has returned. To the father, "...it is enough that he *has* returned."[14] Nolland agrees, noting that upon his return the son is at once the object of his father's "overwhelming compassion."[15] Darrell Bock summarizes succinctly the essence of what is pictured in verse 20b: "Compassion reigns."[16]

The father's compassion, evidenced in 20b recalls Jesus' teaching in Luke 6:36: "Be merciful, just as your Father is merciful." Also, one is reminded of the response of Jesus to the plight of the widow of Nain (7:13), and the good Samaritan's response to the severely wounded traveler (10:33).[17] In commenting on the theme of compassion running through Luke's gospel, Barton observes, "...it is compassion for the lost that brings about life out of death and that makes restoration—even transformation—possible in people's lives."[18]

This scene of reconciliation pictured in Luke 15:20b has been portrayed and interpreted by many artists. Nouwen's seminal monograph on the parable of the Prodigal Son, *The Return of the Prodigal Son: A Story of Homecoming*, is indeed based primarily on Rembrandt's famous painting, rather than the text of Luke itself. Schweizer notes that many painters have rightly understood Luke 15:20 to be the heart of the parable.[19]

In verse 21, the prodigal offers his confession to the father. The son admits his sin; he admits that he has disgraced the father. He goes so far as to offer to forfeit his sonship. Some important Greek manuscripts, as well as the Vulgate, tack on "treat me as one of your hired servants" to the son's confession that he is no longer worthy of the father's paternal love. Other significant manuscripts, however, do not include this addition. Hultgren, among many others, suggests that the additional phrase has been added to correspond with the son's words in 15:19, and that the shorter reading is preferred.[20]

If the shorter reading is indeed preferred, the son may well have intended to include the additional phrase in his confession, but the father interrupts in order to begin the preparations for the celebration of the prodigal's return home. The father calls for the best robe to be put on the young son, for a ring to be placed on his hand, and shoes on his feet. The prodigal's penitential offer of forfeiture of his sonship is immediately and emphatically denied by the father. His *son* has returned, and the marks of sonship are instantly and unconditionally restored. The best robe clearly signifies the son being restored to a place of honor in the family, and recalls the robe of righteousness referred to in Isaiah 61:10. Likewise, the ring unambiguously indicates restoration to sonship, and recalls Genesis 41:42; Esther 3:10, and 8:2, where the giving or possession of a ring symbolizes the recipient's occupying a place of honor. Scholars are nearly universal in noting that in the culture in which the story is cast, servants or slaves typically went barefoot. Shoes were a luxury, and typically a sign of status. On top of the robe and ring, the restoring of shoes to the prodigal confirms his restoration to a place of honor in the family. The father will not have the son barefoot one second longer than is absolutely necessary.

The note of reconciliation struck in verses 20b-22 leads to one of celebration in 23-24. In verse 23a, the father commands that the fatted calf be prepared as part of the celebration of the young son's return home. This is reminiscent of I Samuel 28:24-25, where Saul and his servants are offered hospitality before they go on their way. Meat was not a staple of the diet in the culture in which the parable is set, but a luxury reserved for special celebratory occasions. In 23b-24, the father urges that the celebration begin with feasting and joyful merrymaking, for his son was as good as dead, but now is alive again. Having been lost to his family, the prodigal is now, blessedly, found. Verse 24b makes clear that the celebration does, indeed, begin. Nouwen's widely-read book on the parable of the Prodigal Son is poignantly subtitled: *A Story of Homecoming.*

A. R. C. Leaney observes that the notion of one spiritually 'lost' being regarded as dead and yet capable of being restored to 'life again' is Jewish, as is powerfully shown in Ezekiel 37:1-14.[21] Both 15:24 and 15:32, using the lost/found imagery, link the parable to the similar exclamations of the shepherd and the woman in the preceding parables (15:6,9).[22]

In summary regarding the father's place in Luke 15:20b-24, Brunner asserts that in the person of the father is conveyed the most important message of the parable, "...God's unbelievable love."[23] In his response to the returning prodigal there is: "Not a word of reproach, not one question."[24] There is only love.

Brown interprets this love, a representation of God's love for humanity, to be a love, "...which pursues us from the cradle to the grave..."[25] For Brown, this divine love is, "...the great Christian principle which animates life; not that we first love God, but that He first loves us (I John 4:10)."[26]

Nouwen observes that in the father we see, "...a heart of limitless mercy."[27] This image of the Heavenly Father in 20b-24 makes clear that, regardless of the depths to which one may sink, "...after all is said and done, there is a safe place to return to and receive an embrace."[28]

In Luke 15:20b-24, the reader finds a truly extraordinary portrait of a father representing God's incomprehensibly deep and abiding love. The father's love and mercy toward his humiliated younger son correct our human instincts, which more readily move in the direction of judgment, punishment, and lasting condemnation of a 'prodigal'. In the words of Neil F. Fisher, thanks to the father's boundless love: "In place of a confrontation, the son found a coronation."[29]

As integral as verses 11-20a and 25-32 clearly are to the overall parable, it is in 20b-24 that we find the deepest, most abiding meaning of this multilayered, seemingly inexhaustibly rich story. In the memorable words of Barclay: "In face of a love like that we cannot be other than lost in wonder, love and praise."[30]

Notes

1. Craddock, *Luke*, 187.
2. Hultgren, 86.
3. Donahue, 152.
4. R. Alan Culpepper, "The Gospel of Luke," *The New Interpreter's Bible Volume IX (Nashville: Abingdon, 1995), 302.*
5. Wilfrid Harrington, "The Prodigal Son," *Furrow* 25 (August 1974): 434.
6. Bailey, 47.
7. Drury, 156.
8. Herman Hendrickx, *The Parables of Jesus* (San Francisco: Harper & Row, Publishers, 1986), 154.
9. Hultgren, 86.
10. Bailey, 67.
11. Eduard Schweizer, *The Good News According to Luke.* Tr. David E. Green (Atlanta: John Knox Press, 1984), 249.
12. N. T. Wright, *Jesus and the Victory of God.* Christian Origins and the Question of God, Volume Two (Minneapolis: Fortress Press, 1996), 129.
13. Trench, 407.
14. Plummer, 375.
15. Nolland, 790.
16. Darrell L. Bock, *Luke. Volume 2: 9:51-24:53.* Baker Exegetical Commentary on the New Testament (Grand Rapids: Baker Books, 1996), 1313.
17. Barton, 211.
18. Ibid.
19. Schweizer, 249.
20. Hultgren, 71.
21. A. R. C. Leaney, *The Gospel According to St. Luke.* Harper's New Testament Commentaries. Henry Chadwick, General Editor (New York: Harper & Brothers Publishers, 1958), 218.
22. Hultgren, 80.
23. Brunner, 38.
24. Ibid.
25. Brown, 76.
26. Ibid.
27. Nouwen, 75.
28. Ibid., 138.
29. Neal F. Fisher, *The Parables of Jesus: Glimpses of God's Reign* (New York: Crossroad, 1990), 68.
30. Barclay, *The Gospel of Luke*, 245.

Chapter Three
The Elder Son

"Now his elder son was in the field;
and when he came and approached the house, he heard music and dancing.
He called one of the slaves and asked what was going on.
He replied, 'Your brother has come, and your father has killed the fatted calf,
because he has got him back safe and sound.'
Then he became angry and refused to go in.
His father came out and began to plead with him.
But he answered his father,
'Listen! For all these years I have been working like a slave for you,
and I have never disobeyed your command;
yet you have never given me even a young goat
so that I might celebrate with my friends.
But when this son of yours came back,
who has devoured your property with prostitutes,
you killed the fatted calf for him!'
Then the father said to him,
'Son, you are always with me, and all that is mine is yours.
But we had to celebrate and rejoice,
because this brother of yours was dead and has come to life;
he was lost and has been found.'"

Luke 15:25-32

In interpreting the parable of the Prodigal Son, it is important to recognize verses 25-32 not as an appendage, but as integral to the parable's message of God's amazing love and grace. The love and tenderness of the father evidenced in verses 20-24 are shown in equal measure in 25-32.

At first glance, the elder son would appear to be the complete opposite of the prodigal. He has stayed at home. He is a dutiful worker. He has committed no obvious indiscretion such as the younger son's arrogant and presumptuous leave-taking. To all appearances, the elder son honors the father. Yet as verses 25-32 unfold, we see that the two sons have more in common than is at first obvious. Though the particulars of their actions differ widely, in time it becomes apparent that they both stand in need of their father's deep love, his steadfast forgiveness, and his gracious acceptance.

R. T. Kendall wisely observes that in the elder son we see the "subtlety" of sin.[1] Though outwardly loyal to his father and dutiful, the older brother harbors in his heart anger and self-righteousness.[2] In introducing his commentary on verses 25-32, Trench notes, "...the contrast which shall now be drawn between the large heart of God and the narrow grudging heart of man."[3] In verses 20b-24, the father is the very image of grace. Verses 25-32 present in the person of the elder brother a definitive portrait of an arrogant, self-righteous human being oriented toward exclusivity rather than unity.

Regarding verse 27, Bailey comments that the servant's response to the elder brother's query concerning the music and dancing is "freighted" with meaning.[4] The servant informs the older brother that the younger son has returned and that the father has received him and has called for a celebration. This is, of course, exactly the Pharisees' complaint against Jesus (15:2). Bailey asserts that by this point in the narrative it is "unmistakably clear" that the figure of the father has, "...evolved into a symbol for Jesus himself."[5]

In verse 28a, the elder son refuses to enter the celebration. It is crucial to realize, given the culture in which the parable is set, that such a refusal to accept the invitation by his own father is an extreme insult on the part of the elder son. Bailey notes that in the social situation pictured in the parable, it is incumbent on the male members of the family to at least greet the invited guests. The failure to observe this courtesy is an insult to the guests, as well as the father as host. Bailey asserts: "The older son knows this and thereby his action is an intentional public insult to his father."[6]

Verse 28b makes clear that the father entreats the elder son to come in and join the celebration. The father loves his sons equally and desires that the elder rejoice in the return of his younger sibling. In Plummer's words: "He treats both sons with equal tenderness."[7]

The father's gracious invitation to the elder son is rebuffed. As the narrative continues in verses 29-30, the reader encounters what Wright calls the "sheer self-righteousness" of the elder brother, who demonstrates that, outward appearances notwithstanding, he has no more real respect for his father than the younger son exhibited in his leave-taking.[8] Wright notes the audacity of the elder son who "lectures" his father in front of the guests, then refuses his father's heartfelt plea to join in the celebration.[9] Schweizer agrees with Wright's description of the elder son's self-centeredness, going so far as to assert that in his refusal to join the celebration this son exhibits "rage."[10] In his commentary on 29-30, Hultgren refers to the "painful protest" of the elder son.[11]

The pain the elder son experiences in his brother's homecoming stems, in large part, from his belief that the prodigal is not worthy of such a celebrated return. In the words of Hendrickx: "The elder son's fault is that he derives a claim from his performance..."[12] This son believes that his sonship has been earned, contrary to his disloyal younger sibling whose sudden return is being feted lavishly.[13] The elder son's claim in 29b to have never disobeyed a command of his father serves, in Hultgren's view, as a reference to the Pharisees and scribes present for the telling of the parable (15:2), as the word for command, *éntolé*, can also mean commandment.[14]

Nouwen observes that, though to all appearances loyal and faithful to his father, when confronted with the father's gracious welcome to the prodigal, "...a dark power erupts in him and boils to the surface. Suddenly, there becomes glaringly visible a resentful, proud, unkind, selfish person."[15] Roland J. Faley notes that the older brother, "...suffers from narrowness of vision, an exclusiveness, centered in justice, which allows no room for joy over his brother's return."[16] These characteristics portrayed in the elder son are a clear allusion to the scribes and Pharisees. Bailey comments that, like the younger son earlier in the narrative, the elder son has broken a relationship with his father, though he has not necessarily broken a law. This son proudly affirms that he is loyal, never disobedient. In refusing the invitation to join in the celebration of the prodigal's return, however, he also, "...breaks his father's heart."[17]

Barclay writes that the elder son's whole attitude is that of "contempt."[18] This son represents those who, in their self-righteous judgmentalism of others, forfeit the joy of fellowship with God and with their fellow human beings.[19] Bailey is correct in noting that the elder son's actions in 29-30 exhibit the same tone as the prodigal's actions earlier in the narrative: "'I want mine.'"[20]

As the parable nears its conclusion, it becomes apparent, his outward loyalty notwithstanding, that, in the words of David Wenham, the elder brother is in fact "quite out of tune" with his father because of his rejection of the father's gracious love.[21] This son's self-righteousness, in his own mind a blessing, in reality serves as a barrier between him and true communion with the father. Here one is reminded of Matthew 23:1-36, wherein Jesus repeatedly warns the scribes and Pharisees to amend their self-righteous and judgmental ways.

Eugene S. Wehrli agrees that, despite his spacial proximity to his father, the elder son is, in fact, far from sharing the heart of his father. Although he has had every opportunity to learn to emulate his father, his declining to join in the family celebration of the prodigal's return indicates how far apart he is from the father's mindset of forgiveness and reconciliation.[22]

Interestingly, in his commentary on the parable Leaney takes a different approach to the elder son than the vast majority of commentators. He argues that the elder son's indignation toward the celebration of the prodigal's homecoming is natural, and that, "...it is false to the whole spirit of the story to represent him as a monster of hidden selfishness."[23] Though an interesting viewpoint, and worthy of due consideration, this alternate interpretation does not adequately refute the predominant interpretation that the elder brother serves as a representation of the scribes' and Pharisees' tendencies toward self-righteousness and exclusivism.

In verse 31, the father tries yet again to foster reconciliation between himself and his elder son, and between the two sons themselves. The angry, defiant elder son is assured in no uncertain terms of his father's love. Bailey is correct in noting: "For the second time in the same day the father's response is incredible."[24] For the second time the father exhibits a willingness to endure shame amongst his peers and to offer "self-emptying love" in order to bring about a restoration of family unity.[25] Again referring to the culture in which the story is cast, Bailey asserts: "It is almost impossible to convey the shock that must have reverberated through the banquet hall when the father deliberately left his guests, humiliated himself before all, and went out in the courtyard to try to reconcile his older son."[26]

The parable concludes in verse 32 with the father repeating his statement from verse 24 that his son who was dead is, in fact, alive. Though once lost, he has, blessedly, been found! It is no longer a sheep (verse 7), nor a coin (verse 9), but a precious child who has been restored to full fellowship in the family. Barton argues that the Revised Standard Version and New Revised Standard Version translation of *édei* as "fitting" in verse 32 is too weak. He suggests instead that "necessary" is much more appropriate given the context.[27] The recovery of a lost one *necessitates* a celebration.

In summary regarding verses 25-32, Barclay writes that the elder brother was, in a sense, a good man, "...but his goodness was hard, and unlovely, because he had none of the father's love in his heart."[28] Bailey notes that this son's unwillingness to be reconciled to his younger brother causes him to forfeit fellowship with his father.[29] In Bailey's view: "The man who cannot live with his brother obviously cannot live within the family fellowship; thereby harmony with his father is impossible."[30] Ironically, though he sees himself as righteous vis-à-vis his younger brother, the elder brother is, in Bailey's estimation, "...consumed with envy, pride, bitterness, sarcasm, anger, resentment, self-centeredness, hate, stinginess, self-satisfaction, and self-deception."[31] G. Campbell Morgan writes of the elder son: "He was devoted to his father's law, and he was devoted to his father's service; but he was entirely out of sympathy with his father's heart."[32] Plummer agrees, claiming that this son was doing his duty, but not in a "loving spirit."[33] Comparing the two sons, Plummer suggests, "...self-righteousness and exclusiveness are sinful, and may be as fatal as extravagance and licentiousness."[34]

In his evaluation of what the elder brother represents theologically, Bock cautions, "...activity for God by itself or proximity to him is not the same as knowing him through a relationship grounded in a conscious, humble turning to him."[35] Lenski goes so far as to say that due to his self-righteousness, the elder brother is, "...lost in his own father's house."[36] Kalas observes that, sadly, this son's predisposition to judgmentalism has "robbed" him of life's joy.[37] Similarly, Nouwen states particularly poignantly: "Joy and resentment cannot coexist."[38]

Nouwen's experience as a psychotherapist evidences itself in his evaluation of the elder brother. Like Lenski and others, he uses the term 'lost' in discussing this son who has stayed home yet, in a sense, is as adrift as the prodigal was in leaving home. Nouwen says of the elder son: "Exteriorly he did all the things a good son is supposed to do, but interiorly, he wandered away from his father. He did his duty, worked hard every day, and fulfilled all his obligations but became increasingly unhappy and unfree."[39] Nouwen goes on to ponder: "I wonder which does more damage, lust or resentment? There is so much resentment among the 'just' and the 'righteous'. There is so much judgement, condemnation, and prejudice among the 'saints'. There is so much frozen anger among the people who are so concerned about avoiding 'sin.'"[40] Thinking personally, as well as theologically, Nouwen concludes: "Returning home from a lustful escapade seems so much easier than returning home from a cold anger that has rooted itself in the deepest corners of my being."[41]

Schweizer echoes the majority interpretation regarding the elder son: "He lives—outwardly—with his father but not inwardly."[42] Kalas agrees and submits that the "tragedy" of this son is that he could live a lifetime in his father's house and yet take in so little of his father's spirit.[43] Frederick Danker claims that, though Luke 15:11-32 is most often referred to as the parable of the Prodigal Son, the passage, "...recites not so much the waywardness of a young man who fell on bad times as the vagrancy of a young man whose body stayed home but whose heart was lost in misunderstanding of a father's love."[44]

In his summary comments on verses 25-32, Brunner, applying the parable's lessons to contemporary church life, asserts: "The great sin of the Christian church becomes apparent here: the church as in-group, Christianity as a pious caste, way above the sinners on the wrong side of the track. Judgment is passed on others, in particular on those who confess Christ in other ways."[45] Keith Nickle concurs that the judgmentalism of the elder brother is the key to interpreting the parable's multiple lessons. He writes of the elder brother: "He is like those who are so preoccupied with guarding the boundaries of God's grace they do not notice that with the very act of line-drawing they exclude themselves."[46] Barclay observes that, unfortunately, "...God is more merciful in his judgments than many orthodox people..."[47]

A particularly poignant moment in the story occurs in verse 30, when the elder brother refers to the prodigal as, "this son of yours." In his judgmentalism, the older brother, in effect, refuses to acknowledge that the prodigal is, in fact, his brother. Robert H. Stein states: "The older brother's refusal in the picture part of the parable to acknowledge that the returned son is indeed his 'brother' corresponds well in the reality part of the parable with the Pharisees' refusal to acknowledge the outcasts as brothers."[48] Tannehill agrees with the vast majority of interpreters that in offering the parable to the Pharisees and scribes Jesus, "...wants them to recognize the Jewish outcasts as their kin, as part of the family of Israel, and join in the celebration of their return."[49]

Important to the interpretation of the parable, and to all of Jesus' teachings to the Pharisees and scribes, is the reality that Jesus is not condemnatory of them in any lasting, irreversible sense. Rather, his desire is for them to amend their ways and cease from their tendencies toward exclusivism. Madeleine I. Boucher makes this point well in stating: "The second part of the parable is an invitation to those who have always been faithful. Their faithfulness is recognized by God, and his gifts are theirs, too. They are invited to cease murmuring at the way sinners are received and instead to rejoice in this good news."[50] Charles H. Talbert notes that readers are wise to recognize that they sometimes find themselves in the role of the elder brother and that the parable serves as an open invitation to decide against judgmentalism.[51] Brown reminds readers of the parable: "An unforgiving nature is the ugly sin of an unresponding heart. Forgiveness lies at the very center of the Christian Gospel."[52] Culpepper offers this summary comment on the passage: "The parable shows that those who would live by merit can never know the joy of grace."[53]

Notes

1. R. T. Kendall, *The Complete Guide to the Parables: Understanding and Applying the Stories of Jesus* (Grand Rapids: Chosen Books, 2004), 269.
2. Ibid.
3. Trench, 414.
4. Bailey, 80.
5. Ibid.
6. Ibid., 62.
7. Plummer, 378.
8. N. T. Wright, *Luke for Everyone*. Second Edition (Louisville and London: SPCK and Westminster John Knox Press, 2004), 191.
9. Ibid.
10. Schweizer, 249.
11. Hultgren, 80.
12. Hendrickx, 158.
13. Ibid.
14. Hultgren, 81.
15. Nouwen, 71.
16. Roland J. Faley, "There Was Once a Man Who Had Two Sons...," *The Bible Today* 18 (1965): 1185.
17. Bailey, 85.
18. William Barclay, *The Parables of Jesus* (Louisville: Westminster John Knox Press, 1970), 186.
19. Ibid.
20. Bailey, 85.
21. David Wenham, *The Parables of Jesus*. The Jesus Library. Michael Green, Series Editor (Downers Grove, IL: InterVarsity Press, 1989), 112.
22. Eugene S. Wehrli, *Exploring the Parables* (Philadelphia: United Church Press, 1963), 103.
23. Leaney, 219.
24. Bailey, 82.
25. Ibid.
26. Ibid.
27. Barton, 213.
28. Barclay, *Parables*, 187.
29. Bailey, 85.
30. Ibid.

31. Ibid., 86.

32. G. Campbell Morgan, *The Gospel According to Luke* (Grand Rapids: Fleming H. Revell, 1931), 184.

33. Plummer, 377.

34. Ibid.

35. Darrell L. Bock, *The NIV Application Bible: Luke* (Grand Rapids: Zondervan Publishing House, 1996), 415.

36. Lenski, 818.

37. Kalas, 36.

38. Nouwen, 73.

39. Ibid., 69.

40. Ibid., 71.

41. Ibid., 75.

42. Schweizer, 249.

43. Kalas, 38.

44. Frederick W. Danker, *Jesus and the New Age: A Commentary on St. Luke's Gospel* (Philadelphia: Fortress Press, 1988), 275.

45. Brunner, 39.

46. Keith F. Nickle, *Preaching the Gospel of Luke: Proclaiming God's Royal Rule* (Louisville: Westminster John Knox Press, 2000), 163.

47. Barclay, *Parables*, 244.

48. Robert H. Stein, *Luke.* The New American Commentary, Volume 24 (Nashville: Broadman Press, 2004), 407.

49. Tannehill, 244.

50. Madeleine I. Boucher, *The Parables.* New Testament Message. A Biblical-Theological Commentary. Wilfrid Harrington and Donald Senior, Editors (Wilmington, DE: Michael Glazier, Inc., 1981), 101.

51. Charles H. Talbert, *Reading Luke: A Literary and Theological Commentary on the Third Gospel* (New York: Crossroad, 1982), 151.

52. Brown, 117.

53. Culpepper, 305.

Chapter Four
The Interpretation of Luke 15:11-32 in Broad Outline

In his book *Learning to Dance*, Michael Mayne refers to the parable of the Prodigal Son as: "That most compelling of stories. . . "[1] Using words of their own, countless interpreters of Luke 15:11-32 agree with Mayne's assessment. New Testament scholars, literary critics, and readers in general share a deep and abiding appreciation of this very short story which, despite its relative brevity, is seemingly inexhaustible in meaning. Culpepper writes: "It is no hyperbole to say that this parable is a gem. . ."[2] He goes on to say, ". . . all of its facets deserve to be considered."[3] Here Culpepper speaks to the reality that, though at a surface level the story may seem relatively straightforward and easy to interpret, more determined students of the parable will uncover multiple layers of meaning and practical application within this ancient, yet stunningly fresh teaching.

Bailey asserts unhesitatingly: "The image of God as a compassionate father is here given its finest definition in all of Scripture."[4] Nouwen is correct in observing: "It leaves us face to face with one of life's hardest spiritual choices: to trust or not to trust in God's all-forgiving love."[5] Nouwen claims that all of the gospel is contained in Luke 15:11-32 in that: "Jesus' whole life and preaching had only one aim: to reveal this inexhaustible, unlimited motherly and fatherly love of his God and to show the way to let that love guide every part of our lives."[6]

Perceptive readers of Luke's gospel note that joy is a theme which runs throughout the narrative. Hendrickx goes so far as to hold: "Joy is the password of Luke's gospel."[7] This theme of joy begins to be picked up as early as 1:14 and 2:10 in the birth narratives of John the Baptist and Jesus, respectively. Tannehill notes that Luke 15:11-32 carries forward the connection in Luke between repentance and joy.[8] Luke 5:29-34 makes clear that repentance and forgiveness lead to joy and celebration. Likewise the immediate context of the parable of the Prodigal Son, Luke 15:3-10, clearly links the 'lost' being 'found' with celebration. Hendrickx concludes regarding this theme of joy over the lost being found, ". . . in Luke's formulation, joy is given an imperative character; joy is commanded, and rebellion against God now consists in the refusal of this joy."[9] Building on the theme of good news for the outcasts in chapter 14, Luke 15, in Donahue's words, further issues, ". . . the summons to celebrate meals that shatter conventional norms."[10] Such meals in Luke are characterized by joy and the inclusion of *all* who respond to God's gracious invitation to fellowship.

The unforgettable imagery in 15:11-24 of the prodigal's leave-taking and the father's gracious welcome upon the humiliated young son's return teaches, in Trench's words, ". . . there is no extent of departure from God which precludes a return."[11] The father's unbridled, unconditional embrace of the prodigal upon his return shows us, in Nouwen's terms, ". . . a love that knows no limits."[12] Here we see an image of God's boundless love.[13] This extraordinary image illustrating the depths of God's love for human beings challenges us, in Nouwen's view, to allow ourselves to be loved unconditionally and absolutely without prerequisites.[14]

Regarding the portrait of God's love offered in 15:20b-32, Donahue cautions that the "cultural gap" between the first century and our time softens the "shock" of just how compassionate and forgiving the father is pictured as being in the parable.[15] Donahue reminds readers of the parable that, according to ancient Jewish law, parents of rebellious, non-repentant sons had the right to allow such sons to be stoned (Deuteronomy 21:18-21).[16] Bearing in mind the cultural norms of the first century, the father's deep, extravagantly gracious love for both sons comes even more sharply into focus.

In verses 11-20a, the prodigal son is portrayed as arrogant, presumptuous, then, ultimately, repentant. Verses 25-32 introduce the elder son, portrayed as present, dutiful, yet ultimately self-righteous, judgmental, and, as the narrative draws to a close, as yet unrepentant. Robert Farrar Capon writes that the elder son reminds readers of the futility of trying to make one's own righteousness the basis of one's acceptance by God.[17] Though outwardly their lives are very different, both sons are equally loved by the father for who they are, not for what they do or do not do. The elder son, his presumptions to the contrary notwithstanding, is in no position to stand in judgment of his younger, more overtly sinful brother. Etchells reminds readers that while the parable did indeed challenge directly the Pharisees and scribes of Jesus' day, ". . . it continues to bite wherever, as Emily Brontë once put it, we search the Bible (and the God it declares) for promises to ourselves and curses to our neighbors."[18] Etchells states unequivocally that the teaching of 25-32 is that self-righteousness is, ". . . the enemy of grace."[19] In his summary comments regarding these verses Leaney observes: "With exquisite economy the point is made that the tax-gatherers and sinners are brethren of those who murmur at Jesus' associating with them; this responsibility cannot be shelved by calling the sinner 'this son of yours.'"[20]

Nouwen urges readers of the parable to recognize that the unconditional love offered so graciously to *both* sons teaches followers of Jesus to let go of all tendencies to comparison, rivalry, and competition and to, ". . . surrender to the Father's love."[21] Everyone, regardless of who they are, or what they have done, is invited to "come home," and to enter into the reality that, ". . . in God all people are uniquely and completely loved."[22]

The mercy of the father in the parable recalls Jesus' words earlier in Luke: "Be merciful, as your Father is merciful" (6:36). Jeremias writes that in addressing the self-righteous through the parable, ". . . Jesus says to them: See the greatness of God's love for his lost children, and contrast it with your own joyless, loveless, unthankful, and self-righteous lives. Cease from your loveless ways, and be merciful."[23]

The narrative of the parable draws to a close in verse 32, but the careful reader recognizes that the story does not come to a definitive end. The story closes with the elder son facing a decision whether or not to join in the celebration to which he is warmly invited. Here readers are reminded that, like the elder brother in the parable itself, the scribes and Pharisees of Jesus' own day, as well as students of the parable down through the years are not condemned once and for all but are, in the words of Eugene LaVerdiere, "pastorally addressed."[24] As Bowie puts it, ". . . Jesus portrayed the Pharisaic spirit as it was and is. But there was no harshness in what he said; instead, there was a gentle understanding that might melt an icy self-esteem."[25] It is vital to remember in reading Luke 15:11-32 pastorally: "God is a both/and, not an either/or God: to embrace sinners is not to reject Pharisees."[26] In words reminiscent of those of Jeremias, Harrington writes that Jesus calls upon the Pharisees and scribes, ". . . to cease from their loveless, joyless ways and to rejoice with the rising and the returning."[27]

While the parable begins by focusing on the prodigal, it is crucial to remember that it ends with the focus squarely on the elder brother. George B. Caird asks, did the elder brother continue in his rage? Or, ". . . did he follow the lead of his brother, admit that he had made a fool of himself, and join the festivities?"[28] Caird notes that this question is left unanswered. Jesus' listeners/readers must answer the same question for themselves. In Caird's view: "The parable was told not to offer a generous pardon to the nation's prodigals, but to entreat the respectable Jews to rejoice with God over the restoration of sinners, and to warn them that, until they learnt to do this, they would remain estranged from their heavenly father and pitifully ignorant of his true character."[29]

In the end, this extraordinary story offers an image of a celebration of love, forgiveness, and reconciliation to which *all* are invited, because *all* are equally loved and precious in the eyes of God. Both the tax collectors and sinners of 15:1, and the Pharisees and scribes of 15:2 are children of one Father, and both groups are warmly invited to cherish and abide in his merciful embrace.

Notes

1. Michael Mayne, *Learning to Dance* (London: Darton, Longman and Todd, Ltd., 2001), 168.
2. Culpepper, 304.
3. Ibid.

4. Bailey, 88.
5. Nouwen, 75.
6. Ibid., 109.
7. Hendrickx, 164.
8. Tannehill, 242.
9. Hendrickx, 165.
10. Donahue, 158.
11. Trench, 402.
12. Nouwen, 14.
13. Ibid., 78.
14. Ibid., 14.
15. Donahue, 156.
16. Ibid.
17. Robert Farrar Capon, *The Parables of Grace* (Grand Rapids: William B. Eerdmans Publishing Company, 1988), 144.
18. Etchells, 32.
19. Ibid., 38.
20. Leaney, 219.
21. Nouwen, 81.
22. Ibid.
23. Jeremias, *Rediscovering the Parables*, 104.
24. Eugene LaVerdiere, *Luke*. New Testament Message. Wilfrid Harrington and Donald Senior, Editors (Wilmington, DE: Michael Glazier, Inc., 1980), 204.
25. Bowie, 212.
26. Fred B. Craddock, "Luke." In *Harper's Bible Commentary*. James L. Mays, General Editor (San Francisco: Harper & Row Publishers, 1988), 1034.
27. Harrington, 434.
28. Caird, 184.
29. Ibid.

Part II

Introduction

During his final night with his disciples prior to his arrest, Jesus taught them: "This is my commandment, that you love one another as I have loved you" (John 15:12). Earlier in his ministry, in response to a query regarding which commandment is the greatest, Jesus answered: "The first is, 'Hear, O Israel: the Lord our God, the Lord is one; you shall love the Lord your God with all your heart, and with all your soul, and with all your mind, and with all your strength'. The second is this, 'You shall love your neighbor as yourself'. There is no other commandment greater than these" (Mark 12:29-32). In these teachings, and in others, Jesus makes clear that the heart of his ministry is reconciliation. Reconciliation begins with God's love for humanity, expressed most fully in the person and ministry of Jesus. As the beloved children of God, human beings are invited to receive God's love and grace, and then share His love with their fellow human beings. As the verses above make clear, love of others in response to God's love of humanity is simply a part of what it means to be a Christian. In reflecting on the meaning of Jesus, the apostle Paul teaches:

> So if anyone is in Christ, there is a new creation: everything old has passed away; see, everything has become new! All this is from God, who reconciled us to himself through Christ, and has given us the ministry of reconciliation; that is, in Christ God was reconciling the world to himself, not counting their trespasses against them, and entrusting the message of reconciliation to us. (II Corinthians 5:17-19)

Paul continues: "So we are ambassadors for Christ, since God is making his appeal through us; we entreat you on behalf of Christ, be reconciled to God" (II Corinthians 5:20). Jesus Christ offers to humanity reconciliation with God through the sacrifice of himself on the cross for the sin of the world. Followers of Jesus are called, first, to be reconciled to God, and then to be ministers of reconciliation, making known the love and forgiveness of Jesus. Paul puts it so succinctly, yet so powerfully in Ephesians 2:14: "For he is our peace; in his flesh he has made both groups into one and has broken down the dividing wall, that is, the hostility between us." Receiving, and then sharing the peace of Christ is the very foundation of the Christian life. In *The Book of Common*

Prayer, the ministry of the Church is described thusly, ". . . to restore all people to unity with God and each other in Christ."[1] Here the Church's *primary* mission is understood to be that of reconciliation.

The contention of this book is that the parable of the Prodigal Son has a great deal to teach the Church, as well as the wider world, regarding reconciliation. In each of the three main characters, students of the parable may learn much about what to do, and, in some cases, what not to do, in order to know and to make known the reconciling love of Jesus.

When the subject is considered carefully, it is apparent that each individual is affected, in one way or another, by the need for reconciliation. At our core, human beings long, consciously or subconsciously, for reconciliation with God, a sense of being at peace, and in harmony with one's Creator. Augustine of Hippo articulates this desire so succinctly and so beautifully, ". . . you made us for yourself and our hearts find no peace until they rest in you."[2] The desire to rest in God is the desire to have faith that one is truly loved and accepted by God. Nouwen recognizes that it is a part of human nature to have, ". . . a great desire to be forgiven."[3] Consciously or subconsciously, humans long for the tender embrace the father offers to both sons in the parable. We long for, in Nouwen's words, ". . . an unambiguous sense of safety, a lasting home."[4]

A person of faith's inherent desire to be at peace with God is followed naturally by the need to be reconciled in his or her relationships with others. Reconciliation is an issue in families, where anger, disappointment, and, tragically, sometimes violence has taken the place of love, forgiveness, and trust. Often times there is a clear need for reconciliation among friends and/or co-workers, where a basic, healthy mutual respect has given way to misunderstanding, anger, and a loss of fellowship.

Sadly, too often within congregations, Jesus' unambiguous desire for a community based on love does not square with the reality of the congregation's experience of disunity. The need for reconciliation among Church members is evident at local, regional, denominational, and, indeed, at international levels. It is indeed sad that so often life in the Church does not reflect Jesus' 'new commandment' to love one another in his name.

In all of these crucial areas of life, the parable of the Prodigal Son is relevant. The prodigal, the elder brother, and the father each have so much to teach students of the parable who seek to be faithful to Jesus' call to love one another in response to having been loved so graciously, and so compassionately, by God.

Having reviewed the basic meaning of the parable in broad outline in Part I, we now turn our attention to the specific issue of reconciliation. What does Luke 15:11-32 have to teach regarding reconciliation—the deep, inherent desire to know unity with God and with those whom God unambiguously calls us to love in His name?

Notes

1.   *The Book of Common Prayer* (New York: The Church Hymnal Corporation, 1979), 855.
2.   St. Augustine of Hippo, *Confessions*. Translated, with an Introduction by R. S. Pine-Coffin (New York: Penguin Books, 1961), 21.
3.   Nouwen, 11.
4.   Ibid., 5.

Chapter Five
The Prodigal Son and Reconciliation

Then Jesus said,
"There was a man who had two sons.
The younger of them said to his father,
'Father, give me the share of the property that will belong to me.'
So he divided his property between them.
A few days later the younger son gathered all he had
and traveled to a distant country,
and there he squandered his property in dissolute living.
When he had spent everything, a severe famine took place
throughout that country, and he began to be in need.
So he went and hired himself out to one of the citizens of that country,
who sent him to his fields to feed the pigs.
He would gladly have filled himself with the pods that the pigs were eating;
and no one gave him anything.
But when he came to himself he said,
'How many of my father's hired hands have bread enough and to spare,
but here I am dying of hunger!
I will get up and go to my father, and I will say to him,
"Father, I have sinned against heaven and before you;
I am no longer worthy to be called your son;
treat me like one of your hired hands."'
So he set off and went to his father.

Luke 15:11-20a

In studying the prodigal son from the standpoint of reconciliation, one is reminded of the importance of absolutely honest self-assessment. In seeking reconciliation with another, an individual must be willing to take an honest look at himself or herself, and to examine what role he or she has played in the disunity currently experienced. Such honest self-examination may be uncomfortable, and may not come easily, but it is essential in genuinely seeking to be reconciled with the other(s). Where at least two persons are involved, at least two sides of the story always exist. When disunity characterizes a relationship, each party to the relationship must be willing to recognize and acknowledge the part he or she has played in the breakdown of the relationship.

In the parable, the prodigal son is, without question, guilty of presumptuousness. Early on in the narrative he is a picture of self-centeredness. He clearly lacks the proper regard for his father, and for the rest of his family as well. In the early part of the parable, his actions reflect concern only for himself. His untimely leave-taking will affect each member of his family for as long as they live, yet his concern is only for himself, what *he* wants, what *he* is due.

In separating himself from his family, the prodigal exhibits an immature desire for momentary satisfaction and immediate pleasure. He wants his due *now*, unwilling to wait to receive his proper inheritance at the appropriate time. He has his role to play in the family, yet he wishes to separate himself in order to satisfy his desire for independence and pleasure on his own terms and on his own schedule. The prodigal frames his request for his inheritance in terms of what will be due him. In his view, he simply requests what is rightfully his. But in his presumptuousness, he separates himself from his natural place in the larger family unit.

In seeking reconciliation with another person or persons, we must be willing to take a long, hard look at our own actions. Have we acted presumptuously or selfishly? Have we, perhaps unwittingly, placed our own desires ahead of the needs of the larger group? However uncomfortable such introspection may be, any genuine reconciliation is dependent upon our willingness to be honest with ourselves, and with others, regarding the role we ourselves have played in allowing estrangement to take the place of unity.

Verse 17 is crucial to understanding the full import of the parable. Here it is made clear that the prodigal does, in fact, take a good, hard look at himself and his situation. As is stated in the parable, "... he came to himself..." In John 8:32 Jesus teaches, ". . . and you will know the truth, and the truth will make you free." Having hit rock bottom, the prodigal acknowledges the truth of his situation. He has made a terrible mistake. He is truly in a foreign country in the deepest sense of that word. He belongs at home. His leave-taking was premature and wholly selfish. Acknowledging the reality of his desperate plight, he comes to himself. He remembers who he is. He remembers *whose* he is. In coming to himself, he reclaims his true identity as the beloved son of his father. He reclaims his true identity as a member of a loving family, a family in which he holds a rightful, honored place. Blessedly, rather than remaining in a state of defiant self-centeredness, the prodigal has the wisdom to come to himself, to come to his senses, and to courageously determine: "I will get up and go to my father, and I will say to him, 'Father, I have sinned against heaven and before you . . .'" (Luke15:18). In verse 20a, we see that the prodigal follows through. He has the courage of his convictions. He is willing to repent. In returning home, the prodigal confesses the error of his ways. He has the humility to admit that he has made a terrible mistake. Having chosen to go to a foreign country, the prodigal now comes to realize where home truly is. He now knows that he does not belong by himself, isolated from those who love him. He has truly come to himself. He longs for home. His arrogance is gone. He is no longer defiant. He now desires his true and lasting inheritance—to be reunited with his father. "So he set off and went to his father" (Luke 15:20a).

It takes more courage to admit having made a serious mistake, than to remain defiant in our isolation. True reconciliation requires us to give as well as receive. The truth does, in fact, set us free. Admitting one's own part in the breakdown of the relationship opens the door to reclaiming one's rightful place in the relationship. Having served as a model of arrogant self-centeredness, the prodigal, in the end, models one of the most important steps in the journey toward reconciliation. He teaches the importance of absolute honesty, of a heartfelt repentance, and of the willingness to take the first steps in the journey back home to a relationship characterized by love rather than by alienation.

In addition to his example regarding honest introspection and repentance, the prodigal's story reminds us that in relationships we simply must take into account the perspectives and feelings of others. The prodigal's self-centered leave-taking affects not only himself, but his entire family. If we belong to a larger group, then in considering our actions we are obliged to consider their effects on those with whom we are in relationship. In enjoying the benefits of belonging to a larger group, obligations regarding our place in the group and the group's overall health and well-being must be considered. In taking his leave from the family, the prodigal fails to recognize what he is giving up. Once in a foreign country, however, and having gained the independence he once sought, he realizes that he is truly alone. By leaving home, he has lost so much more than he has gained. Fortunately, he comes to himself, both recognizing and acknowledging his terrible mistake. He then has the courage to return home to the loving family in which he rightfully belongs.

When a relationship breaks down, it is very easy to focus on the role others have played in the loss of unity. It is all too tempting to throw stones at those who may well have participated, and are in some way responsible for, the growing estrangement in the relationship. Yet the prodigal teaches us not to be too hasty in throwing stones. An honest assessment of his place in the parable reminds us to be willing to come to ourselves, to be willing to take an honest inventory of our own thoughts and actions and to be willing to examine the role we have played in growing apart from those whom Jesus calls us to love.

Chapter Six
The Compassionate Father and Reconciliation

But while he was still far off,
his father saw him and was filled with compassion;
he ran and put his arms around him and kissed him.
Then the son said to him,
'Father, I have sinned against heaven and before you;
I am no longer worthy to be called your son.'
But the father said to his slaves,
'Quickly, bring out a robe—the best one—and put it on him;
put a ring on his finger and sandals on his feet.
And get the fatted calf and kill it, and let us eat and celebrate;
for this son of mine was dead and is alive again;
he was lost and is found!'
And they began to celebrate.

Luke 15:20b-24

For persons wishing to be faithful, effective reconcilers, it is a given that such persons must first genuinely desire reconciliation. Christians seeking reconciliation are called to embrace Jesus' command to love one another (John 15:12). Our commitment to be reconcilers begins, in large part, by accepting the apostle Paul's teaching that Jesus Christ himself has given us the ministry of reconciliation (II Corinthians 5:18-20). In the parable of the Prodigal Son, the father offers people of faith the perfect model of what it means to be a reconciler. The father shows us the depths of love, compassion, forgiveness, and grace that Christians are called to offer others in the name of Jesus.

In verse 20b, we see that the father was not waiting passively for his young son to return home. Instead the father is looking for his son. While the prodigal is still off in the distance, the father sees him and is filled with compassion. A heart for reconciliation begins with a predisposition to compassion. More than anything, the father in the parable teaches in a most compelling way that fundamental to the life of faith is a compassionate spirit. He is the embodiment of God's compassionate, grace-filled love, and our calling as Christians is not only to receive this compassionate love but to learn to offer this gift from God to others.

Before the prodigal has a chance to offer his repentance, the father, *filled* with compassion, runs to his young son and embraces him and kisses him. Here we see divine love. Here we see grace. The prodigal is loved not conditionally, but compassionately; not reservedly, but fully. We have so much to learn from this one moment: "But while he was still far off, his father saw him and was filled with compassion; he ran and put his arms around him and kissed him" (Luke 15:20b). Nouwen reminds readers that the Father is always looking for his children with outstretched arms in order to receive them back into his embrace and to whisper in their ears: "'You are my Beloved, on you my favor rests.'"[1]

In his interpretation of this part of the parable, Nouwen claims that: "Becoming like the heavenly Father is not just one important aspect of Jesus' teaching, it is the very heart of his message."[2] We as sinful human beings will always find ourselves in the position of needing to return to the Father; however, as Nouwen observes: "The return to the Father is ultimately the challenge to become the Father."[3] Of course, human beings will never do this perfectly. Still, persons of faith are called to learn more and more how to offer love and grace toward their sisters and brothers rather than judgment and condemnation.

In Luke 6:36, Jesus teaches: "Be merciful, just as your Father is merciful." Nouwen holds that this is the "core" message of the gospel, and is: "Perhaps the most radical statement Jesus ever made. . ."[4] In this teaching Jesus is actually inviting us to become like God, and to offer to others the same compassion that we have been so graciously offered.[5] Nouwen challenges us to understand that as a Christian, one's, ". . . final vocation is indeed to become like the Father and to live out his divine compassion in . . . daily life."[6] He asserts: "Though I am both the younger son and the older son, I am not to remain them, but to become the Father."[7] In imitating the father, we are seeking to be, ". . . looking at people and this world through the eyes of God."[8]

As we learn to cultivate a heart of compassion, we learn the lesson the father teaches us in the parable. Though as human beings we will always be able to identify with both the younger and the elder son, we are at the same time called not to remain content with this reality, but to grow more and more into the image of the father, not in terms of moral perfection, but rather in terms of being characterized by a desire to offer others a response of compassionate love and a genuine desire for reconciliation rather than a spirit of judgmentalism and self-righteousness.

In verse 21, the prodigal confesses his sin and offers the father his repentance. He goes so far as to offer to forfeit his rights and privileges as his father's child, thinking, ". . . I am no longer worthy to be called your son." But the father will have none of this regarding the son's willingness to forfeit his rightful place in the family. It is crucial to note here that the younger son has indeed confessed his sin. He has offered repentance. Yet in verses 22-24 we see that the father's response is not condemnation, nor punishment, but grace. The prodigal's sonship is immediately validated. The prodigal is re-clothed in the trappings of an honored son. The father in no uncertain terms welcomes the prodigal back into the family, unconditionally. The father's heart is geared toward reconciliation, not judgment and lingering alienation. The father's desire is for his young son to be in the family, not marginalized, on the outside looking in. The father's joy is palpable in verse 24. A beloved child is reclaimed The family is once again whole. In the father's loving response to his young son, there is so much for us to learn. Jesus' commandment to his disciples is unambiguous. We are to love one another. In the parable of the Prodigal Son, the father shows what this means. As we consider our role in the ministry of reconciliation, the crucial question for us to ask is: "What would the Father have us do?"

In considering carefully the lessons of Luke 15:20b-24, one is reminded of the necessity to receive forgiveness when it is offered. A heartfelt invitation to reconciliation is an invitation to be accepted gratefully and joyfully. Nouwen is correct in recognizing that for human beings, a belief in total, absolute forgiveness does not come readily.[9] For prideful people who, consciously or subconsciously, believe that restoration has to be earned by right actions, ". . . truly accepting love, forgiveness, and healing is often much harder than giving it."[10] He asserts that one of the greatest challenges of the spiritual life is to receive God's forgiveness freely, as: "There is something in us humans that keeps us clinging to our sins and prevents us from letting God erase our past and offer us a completely new beginning."[11] When he comes to himself and decides to return home to his father, the prodigal releases his prideful self-centeredness and his presumptions regarding his own ability for self-determination. He has hit rock bottom and recognizes his need of the father's love. In his helplessness to pull himself out of his self-created pit, the prodigal teaches careful students of the parable that: "Receiving forgiveness requires a total willingness to let God be God and to do all the healing, restoring, and renewing."[12]

Notes

1. Nouwen, 44.
2. Ibid., 125.
3. Ibid., 123.
4. Ibid.
5. Ibid.
6. Ibid., 121.
7. Ibid.
8. Ibid., 17.
9. Ibid., 52.
10. Ibid., 13.
11. Ibid., 53.
12. Ibid.

Chapter Seven
The Elder Son and Reconciliation

Now his elder son was in the field;
and when he came and approached the house, he heard music and dancing.
He called one of the slaves and asked what was going on.
He replied, 'Your brother has come,
and your father has killed the fatted calf,
because he has got him back safe and sound.'
Then he became angry and refused to go in.
His father came out and began to plead with him.
But he answered his father,
'Listen! For all these years I have been working like a slave for you,
and I have never disobeyed your command;
yet you have never given me even a young goat
so that I might celebrate with my friends.
But when this son of yours came back,
who has devoured your property with prostitutes,
you killed the fatted calf for him!'
Then the father said to him,
'Son, you are always with me, and all that is mine is yours.
But we had to celebrate and rejoice,
because this brother of yours was dead and has come to life;
he was lost and has been found.'

Luke 15:25-32

Having experienced the loving and grace-filled response of the father in verses 20-24, we meet the elder brother in verses 25-32. His response to the prodigal's return is the opposite of the father's. In studying the parable from the standpoint of reconciliation, the elder son has much to teach us. Contrary to the father, the reaction of his elder son is a picture of what not to do if we are to take to heart the ministry of reconciliation.

We meet the elder son in the field, at his post working, doing what is expected of him. He becomes aware of an unexpected celebration taking place in the house. A servant informs him that the celebration is in honor of the younger son's return home. In verse 28, we see that the elder son becomes angry and refuses to go in to the party. That he becomes angry so quickly and in such depth that he refuses to join in the celebration indicates his underlying resentment toward his younger brother. Herein lies a key point in studying the parable with a view to reconciliation. Contrary to his father's predisposition to love and compassion, we see in the elder brother an underlying resentment and anger toward his younger sibling. The elder son has clearly separated himself from his brother. Though they are family, mutual love and respect has given way to estrangement. From the elder brother's perspective, the commonality he naturally shares with his sibling is no longer the focus of the relationship. Alienation now characterizes his feelings toward his brother; hence, he responds to news of the prodigal's return with anger, not love.

Despite the father's pleading, the elder son refuses to repent of his anger. In verse 29, we see the elder son's underlying resentment toward his father come to the surface. He says: "For all these years I have been working like a slave for you. . ." Here we see the underlying, heretofore unspoken resentment. This son is dutiful. Outwardly, he is loyal and dependable. Yet in his heart there is anger. His apparent faithfulness is not offered out of love, but out of a joyless sense of duty. Though to all appearances the 'good son', he is, in reality, no nearer his father's heart than the wayward prodigal.

The elder son has so much to teach us here. To be faithful to Jesus' commandment to love, his followers must cultivate a spirit predisposed to love and to joy. We must recognize sisters and brothers as just that—sisters and brothers, equals, whom we are called to love. The elder son sees himself over against his brother rather than as one with him. Those who call themselves Christians are called to remember that followers of Jesus are friends in him, not enemies! Though persons of faith will inevitably face significant disagreement on matters of genuine importance, our underlying predisposition is to be one of love toward one another, not resentment. Christians are to experience a sense of being one in Jesus, knowing themselves to be equally loved, equally forgiven, and continuously called to the ministry of reconciliation in response to Jesus' unambiguous command to love one another (John 15:12). There is so much joy to be found in the younger son's return home. Sadly, the elder son chooses the opposite.

In verse 30a, the elder son refers to his brother as, ". . . this son of yours. . ." A reconciling heart would be predisposed to recognize the prodigal as 'my brother'. The ministry of reconciliation is, ultimately, a call to unity. Unity does not necessarily connote exact sameness. It certainly does not connote easy agreement on all matters. Still, surely those who confess that Jesus is Lord have more in common than that which is divisive. It is what we share in common, the love and grace of Jesus Christ, that we are called to share with one another. Both sons in the parable share equally in the father's love. It is that love which is their common bond, the ground of their relationship, and therein lies their hope for reconciliation. Here again we are reminded of Jesus' own words: "This is my commandment, that you love one another as I have loved you" (John 15:12). Though at points Christians may disagree deeply with one another, still the call is clear to recognize in each other the oneness shared in proclaiming Jesus as Lord. As the apostle Paul puts it so succinctly, yet so powerfully in Ephesians

2:14: "For he is our peace; in his flesh he has made both groups into one and has broken down the dividing wall, that is, the hostility between us" (Ephesians 2:14). In his reaction to the prodigal's return, the elder son is content to recognize the dividing wall between the siblings. The father's desire, however, is for the two sons to be reunited through his equal love, and his equal tenderness toward both children.

In verse 30b, the elder son accuses the prodigal of wasting his inheritance on prostitutes. Based on the contents of the parable, this is an assumption on the part of the elder brother. In his anger, in his alienation from his younger brother, the elder has become accusatory. He is assigning to his younger sibling motives and actions he may or may not have had. In considering the work of reconciliation, it is crucial to recognize and to remember that one cannot truly know another's mind or heart. One never knows for certain another's thoughts. We do not know someone else's motives. We have not experienced someone else's life journey. In working toward reconciliation in a mature and effective way, we simply cannot prejudge another person's attitude or actions. True reconciliation requires a genuine openness to someone else's thoughts and experiences. Openness in this case does not imply an easy agreement. Rather than the resentment and anger of the elder brother, however, we are called, remembering Nouwen's words, to be more like the father.

Verses 31-32 offer us once again the picture of the loving father. Having loved the prodigal with an amazing gracefulness, the same love is now offered equally to the elder son. Here we see the same tenderness. In the eyes of the father, the elder son's resentment is no better or no worse that the prodigal's presumptuousness. To the father, one child is not better than the other. Though clearly different in temperament and behavior, each son is equally loved, equally cherished by the father. For the family to be complete, each child is invited to live in the same house, to take his rightful place in the family, and to share equally in the father's gracious love. Verse 32 makes it unmistakably clear that to celebrate the prodigal's return in no way grants him favored status as opposed to the elder son. In the younger son's return there is a reunion. He was, ". . . lost and has been found." The younger son is experiencing reconciliation. In his return, unity is overcoming estrangement. Alienation is replaced by a loving, accepting embrace. The elder son is invited to share in the celebration. The father desires for all of his children to know his love, and to rekindle their love for one another. This is, ultimately, the ministry of reconciliation—to know, and to share, God's love and peace.

Conclusion

In his contribution to Simon Wiesenthal's *The Sunflower*, Theodore M. Hesburgh refers to the parable of the Prodigal Son as: "The greatest story of Jesus . . ."[1] Hesburgh certainly is not alone in his assessment of Luke 15:11-32. Mayne writes that Jesus uses the parable to illustrate, ". . . what for many, in the detail of the father going out to greet and embrace his returning child, is the most powerful analogy of that gracious acceptance of the ever-forgiving God."[2] Commentators agree that one of the chief reasons the Prodigal Son is frequently judged to be one of, if not the most significant and beloved teachings of Jesus is that it is as fresh and as applicable in the present as when first told nearly 2,000 years ago, and that it will remain so indefinitely. Mayne observes that the parable of the Prodigal Son, along with the parable of the Good Samaritan, speaks, ". . . powerfully of my relationship with God, and the nature of compassion and forgiveness; truths which touch me deeply and will be as relevant for our children's children as they were for their first hearers."[3] Basil Hume agrees with his contemporary, Mayne, on the abiding significance of Luke 15:11-32, writing: "Out of the many texts of Scripture that we could select to talk about God's search for man, there is one which is deeply moving: the story of the prodigal son."[4]

Along with Wiesenthal's *The Sunflower*, Miroslav Volf's *Exclusion and Embrace* is recognized as one of the seminal works on reconciliation. In his book, Volf recognizes the parable of the Prodigal Son as being, ". . . the profound and singularly fecund story. . ." in the New Testament.[5] Indeed, Volf acknowledges that *Exclusion and Embrace* in its entirety is but an attempt to draw out the full "social significance" of Luke 15:11-32.[6]

The subtitle of the present work is, *The Parable of the Prodigal Son and Reconciliation*. The thesis of this work is that Luke 15:11-32 is essential to a biblically-based theology of reconciliation. W. Mark Richardson concurs with the contention of this book when he states: "There is no domain untouched by the need for reconciliation."[7] The particular claim of this present work is that no area of reconciliation, be it personal or corporate, local or global, need be left untouched by the inexhaustibly rich and seemingly universally applicable parable of the Prodigal Son. Any biblically based theology of reconciliation is wise to be founded on, remembering Hesburgh's words, the greatest story of Jesus.

The parable of the Prodigal Son has profound and lasting implications for reconciliation, whether the issue at hand is framed in personal, theological, political, or sociological terms. Pheme Perkins wisely notes that the parable serves not simply as an example for individuals, but, ". . . as a challenge to the community of disciples. Can they exhibit such reconciliation?"[8] People of faith are challenged by the parable to learn the wisdom of a healthy humility, and the importance of absolutely honest introspection and repentance. As clearly and as compellingly as any story in the Bible, the parable illustrates the centrality of love and compassion and their foundational role in a life of faith. Further, in Luke 15:11-32 readers see unambiguously clear teaching regarding the ever-present temptation to be judgmental and condemnatory when the more spiritually healthy response is the desire for reconciliation and unity.

Michael Battle contends that, ". . . until Christians understand reconciliation as our primary work in the world, we will never understand Christian identity."[9] Battle concurs with Desmond Tutu's assertion that the central teaching of the Christian faith is that in the person of Jesus Christ God has effected reconciliation.[10] Tutu, with whom Battle has traveled extensively, reminds followers of Jesus that in him, ". . . we are given the glorious ministry of reconciliation."[11]

Titus Presler is correct in reminding Christians, ". . . any human work of reconciliation has its source in God's reconciling the world to God in Christ (2 Cor. 5:16-21)."[12] A biblically-based theology of reconciliation is necessarily grounded in the remembrance that it is Jesus himself who, in Tutu's term, effected reconciliation with God and makes reconciliation in the name of God possible. Ann Belford Ulanov agrees with Presler, noting that biblically-based reconciliation, " . . . opens into a country of peace. It opens our attention toward another source in which we live and move and find our being."[13]

The character of the father in Luke 15:11-32 represents God primarily, yet he also functions to remind readers of the mission of Jesus himself. Johnson notes that the father's, ". . . mercy and openness to both children stands as the emblem of Jesus' prophetic mission from God to restore the people with an open invitation to all."[14] The image of the kingdom of God portrayed in the parable is one of unity, one of reconciliation rather than lasting division. In the words of Bernard Brandon Scott: "The father does not reject. The metaphor for the kingdom is the father's coming out, both for the younger son and for the elder."[15] Importantly, David Bryan Hoopes cautions that reconciliation among Christians in particular is not an end in itself. The Church is to be concerned with reconciliation at a global level. The reconciling love of Jesus is to make, ". . . the Church a place of communion for all."[16] Along these lines Battle quotes Dom Helder Camara's reminder that as a Christian: "My door, my heart, must be open to everyone, absolutely everyone."[17] In addressing the parable of the Prodigal Son to the Pharisees and scribes, Jesus does not seek to condemn them lastingly or unalterably, but to turn their hearts to be more embracing of all of God's children.

When speaking of the parable's teaching on forgiveness and reconciliation, one is well advised to avoid using such terms glibly. Luke 15:11-32 addresses these issues in a deeply profound way. Both sons, each in their own way, exhibit behavior that is as deeply insulting to the father as was possible in the culture in which the story is cast. Writing out of his experiences in South Africa, Tutu wisely cautions that forgiveness and reconciliation are not, ". . . something to be entered into lightly, facilely."[18] He reminds us that: "True reconciliation is not cheap. It cost God the death of His only begotten Son."[19] Mayne observes similarly: "Forgiveness is complex and often painfully hard; if it were not, it would have no power to be life-changing."[20] Acknowledging the difficulty of true reconciliation in circumstances of deep division, Battle writes that reconciliation, ". . . is hard work, hard work that is active and that threatens to challenge and change worldviews. . . "[21] This is precisely what Jesus attempts to help his critics, the Pharisees and scribes addressed directly in 15:2, to realize. His desire is for their worldview, which is predisposed toward seeing themselves as righteous and others as outside of the true family of God, to be transformed, reoriented toward compassion and inclusion. Along these lines Richardson comments, ". . . in the conditions of nature and history, we find the path toward reconciliation complex and difficult. It involves a change of heart, serious self-examination, the painful task of breaking habits of action in our relations and establishing new ones, and letting go of false certainties."[22]

In the parable, Jesus pictures a scene of genuine reconciliation between the father and his younger son. This son is unconditionally forgiven and welcomed back into the family with no strings attached. The father offers such reconciliation to his older son as well, in absolutely equal measure. The father's love for both sons is unbridled, extravagant in its graciousness and comprehensiveness. Rowan Williams writes that in speaking of reconciliation, as the word is used in talking of personal relations, or, in a more explicitly theological context, in speaking of one's relationship with God, it, ". . . normally suggests authentically fresh possibilities, new beginnings, not a temporary cease-fire in a situation that remains basically unchanged."[23] The father offers such reconciliation in Luke 15:11-32.

At first glance, the prodigal son appears to be one of the most tragic figures in all of literature. Initially, he is the definitive embodiment of arrogance and self-centeredness. He offers his father the ultimate insult—in effect, wishing the father were dead. Once he has received his inheritance early and taken leave to a foreign country, he experiences the depths of deprivation and humiliation. In the foreign country, the prodigal hits rock bottom. He is utterly alone in the deepest sense of that term. And yet, ultimately, all is not lost. The prodigal, who is as good as dead in the foreign country, will rise to newness of life through the grace of his father.

John Claypool, in his classic work, *Tracks of a Fellow Struggler*, remarks: "God wants us to become mature sons and daughters."[24] What readers see, in part, in Luke 15:11-32 is the beginning of the prodigal's journey into maturity. Battle reminds his readers that we are to be, ". . . lifelong students of God."[25]

Along the way, Battle notes, we learn humility.[26] John O'Donohue observes that: "The human journey is a continuous act of transfiguration."[27] In the parable, we see the early steps in the prodigal's journey toward being transformed. Equally importantly, readers also see the father's invitation to his elder son to a new way of life.

Reflecting on the prodigal's premature leave-taking, Culpepper states: "Unfortunately, we usually learn to demand our rights before we learn to value our relationships."[28] Though from a strictly legal point of view the prodigal was within his rights to request his share of the inheritance, in so doing he severs relationships not only with his father, but with his entire family and the wider community to which he belongs. In considering Luke 15:11-32 from the standpoint of reconciliation, it is crucial to see the implications of the parable regarding maintaining and nurturing relationships. The prodigal and the elder son model the dangers in cutting oneself off from relationships. The prodigal leaves his family, and ultimately finds himself to be starkly alone. The elder son cuts himself off from his younger brother overtly, and then from his father more subtly. It is the father who models the importance of maintaining relationships. Though both sons humiliate him, he never turns his back on either of them but invites them both to return to their rightful home.

Verse 17 of the parable pictures the prodigal coming to his senses. It is one of the key points in the narrative. In her memoir, *An American Childhood*, Annie Dillard writes: "What is important is anyone's coming awake."[29] What one sees in Luke 15:17 and in the verses which follow is the beginning of the prodigal's awakening to who, and whose he really is. We see in the prodigal's coming to himself a repentance, *metánoia*, a turning around. Desmond Tutu wisely observes: "It is never easy to say, 'I am sorry;' they are the hardest words to articulate in any language."[30] Yet the prodigal summons the courage to say to his father in verse 21: "Father, I have sinned against heaven and before you. . ." Volf notes that the prodigal's return home begins not with repentance, but, ". . . with something that makes the repentance possible—the memory of sonship. There is no coming to oneself without the memory of belonging."[31]

From the initial images of the prodigal's destitution in a foreign land, the narrative of the parable moves to images of his restoration. Sam Keen writes in *Fire In the Belly* that one of the standard themes in mythology is, ". . . the promise of the wounded healer."[32] This is, of course, the term that Nouwen has made commonplace. Keen writes further: "In our hurt lies the source of our healing. The bird with the broken and mended wing soars the highest. Where you stumble and fall, there you find the treasure."[33] Referring to the imagery of Luke 15:11-32 itself, Keen notes: "Emerging from the long journey into the shadow of the self the prodigal son returns to a world that was never his home until he wandered far from it."[34] Here one is reminded of Volf's observation that before he can repent the prodigal must reclaim a sense of belonging, a sense of sonship. Even though he is willing to forfeit his rights as the father's son, he nonetheless realizes in his desolation that he is in fact his father's son; he comes to himself, and determines to return to his rightful home.

Upon returning home, the prodigal, rather than forfeiting his place in his father's household, is embraced with open arms. Instead of condemnation, he experiences mercy, forgiveness, and reconciliation. Hume states succinctly: "It is beautiful to receive God's forgiveness, and it is there for the taking."[35] Commentators agree that in the prodigal's reunion with his father we see one of, if not the most, defining instances of forgiveness in all of the Bible. In his memoir, *Telling Secrets*, Frederick Buechner observes, ". . . what we hunger for perhaps more than anything else is to be known in our full humanness, and yet that is often just what we also fear more than anything else."[36] The prodigal returns home to his father in penitence, in contrition, willing to forfeit his rights of sonship due to his sin. Yet his father sees the prodigal in his full humanness and welcomes him home without conditions. We see here a definitive image of God's willingness to see us in our full humanness, as we are in our sinful state, and yet God's response is mercy, boundless forgiveness—grace. Buechner goes on to counsel: "Unclench the fists of your spirit and take it easy."[37] He finishes this line of thought with: "Know that you are precious."[38] The message of the father to both sons is, 'You are precious'. 'You are precious, as you are'.

Similarly to Buechner, Hume urges: ". . . just remember the simple truth, God is in love with you."[39] With the imagery of Luke 15:11-32 informing his thinking, he continues: "If that thought now begins to be part of your thinking, then you will change and so will your life. You will find that peace which nothing can take away from you."[40] The imagery of the parable of the Prodigal Son reminds readers that in the mind of God each individual is, ". . . a specially chosen person, very precious and always loved with a tremendous intensity on the part of God."[41] Hume asks the question: "When does the love of God begin to take over the mastery of our lives?"[42] He answers: "It is surely when we recognize the power and intimacy of God's love for us."[43] Such knowledge comes, in large part, from the extraordinary portrait of God's extravagant love for His children in Luke 15:11-32.

Mayne agrees with Hume's emphasis on learning to see oneself as precious in the eyes of God. He writes that the need to be affirmed, to recognize one's own value, one's belovedness in the eyes of God, is, ". . . part of what it means to be human."[44] He continues: "There are few better nouns to describe the ministry of Jesus of Nazareth than 'affirmation.'"[45] This affirmation does not deny one's sinfulness. It does, however, point to God's grace, witnessed to so powerfully by Luke 15:11-32. Even in our sinfulness, our full humanness, we are loved by God with, to use Hume's term, tremendous intensity. As Mayne puts it: "Once you are persuaded that you are lovable, it changes the way you see everything: God, yourself, your neighbour."[46] Recalling the grace-filled reunion of the prodigal and the father in the parable, Rick Mathis writes that the "real issue" in the spiritual life, ". . . is to live as one who has been found by God."[47]

Regarding our own belovedness in the eyes of God, many followers of Jesus find it difficult to embrace the reality of the gospel's promise of unconditional forgiveness. At a depth level, for many it is difficult to embrace the reality that we are, indeed, God's beloved. In encouraging readers to receive God's love for them, Buechner writes: "We are commanded to love our neighbors as ourselves, and I believe that to love ourselves means to extend to those various selves that we have been along the way the same degree of compassion and concern that we would extend to anyone else."[48] Hugh Prather concurs with Buechner's emphasis on having compassion for oneself. Prather counsels: "Be gentle with yourself, for gentleness is of God, your Father."[49] O'Donohue writes: "When you forgive yourself, the inner wounds begin to heal. You come in out of the exile of hurt into the joy of inner belonging."[50]

In studying the many facets of Luke 15:11-32, one of its major teachings is to remind readers of the centrality of compassion to the life of faith. The father serves as a defining image of compassion. One hopes that through his experience of being lost, then found, that the prodigal would emerge as a much more mature, a much more compassionate figure. Contrary to the father, the elder son demonstrates a marked lack of compassion and is instructive to students of the parable in his own right as a model we are not to emulate. In his book, *A Year Lost and Found*, in which Mayne reflects on his experiences of being afflicted by a form of chronic fatigue syndrome, he observes, ". . it is good if we learn from our own experience of suffering or bereavement, and as a result are wiser, more tolerant, above all more compassionate."[51] Buechner is correct in saying that there is pain in every life, even the apparent luckiest, and that, ". . . buried griefs and hurtful memories are part of us all."[52] In the words of O'Donohue: "One of the great fruits of suffering is compassion. When you have felt and experienced pain, it refines the harshness that may be in you."[53] He recalls Tolstoy's poignant claim that our great duty as human beings is to sow the seed of compassion in each other's hearts.[54]

In his essay in *The Sunflower*, Franz König asserts: "The question of whether there is a limit to forgiveness has been emphatically answered by Christ in the negative."[55] Such sentiments are informed, in no small part, by the unforgettable imagery in Luke 15:11-32 of the father's boundless love for both sons. Hesburgh writes that one of the challenges of faith is: "Can we aspire to be as forgiving of each other as God is of us?"[56] The parable informs the statement: "When you look at someone with eyes of love, you see a reality differently from that of someone who looks at the same person without love, with hatred or even just indifference."[57]

In speaking of compassion, Williams argues: "What makes human life significant, more than animal? Not clothing, not the acquisition of coverings for the naked ego, but the conscious participation in an order of compassion. . ."[58] In his view, ". . . the rationale of the Church's life is irreducibly a matter of showing the results of an act of divine reconciliation in terms of a distinctive kind of human community."[59] Such a statement is grounded in the parable of the Prodigal Son, wherein we see a defining image of divine reconciliation in the prodigal's reunion with his father and a call to a distinctive kind of human community in the father's urging the elder son to join in the celebration of his brother's return.

Hume acknowledges that, for him, Luke 15:11-32 is of singular importance in informing his understanding of the depths of God's love for humanity. He states, in reflecting on the reality that God is love: "These three words are the key to true religion."[60] For Hume the spiritual life is, ". . . an adventure of love."[61] God is, in the end for Hume: "The One who will understand, who will forgive, who will console."[62] With Luke 15:11-32 squarely in the background, Hume shares: "For me personally, the most profound truth of my faith is that there is Someone who loves me completely and totally in spite of my weaknesses and failures. That keeps me going."[63]

Hesburgh's understanding of God is grounded in the understanding that God is, ". . . the great forgiver of sinful humanity."[64] Such a view is informed by the parable of the Prodigal Son. Mayne argues that for humans the most powerful action in the world is, ". . . an unembittered readiness to forgive."[65] Such an understanding is also grounded in the imagery of Luke 15:11-32. Mayne goes so far as to say, ". . . the readiness to forgive and be forgiven is the most powerful weapon in the whole armoury of love."[66]

Hume states succinctly: "When we love we want to forgive."[67] Keen challenges his readers to grapple with the question: "How much does the desire to be a more loving person figure in your life?"[68] For Keen, while love may be partly "grace" or "chemistry," it is also an "art" that must be learned, and: "It takes years of practice to develop a skillful heart."[69] In the parable, the elder brother is being challenged to open his mind and heart to his younger brother and to learn how to be more loving rather than judgmental.

Similarly to Keen, Battle writes: "Just as people have to learn to weave, to write, to do carpentry, each of us needs to learn how to be reconciling and then to practice those skills."[70] In Battle's view, learning to be more loving and practicing reconciliation, ". . . puts skin on God."[71] In discussing the challenge to be more loving, it is crucial to recall that a part of that journey is to learn how to be more loving toward oneself. Mayne reminds his readers, ". . . compassion, like charity, begins at home. It is a kind of blasphemy to view ourselves with so little compassion when God views us with so much."[72] Such a reminder is based in no small measure on Luke 15:11-32, which Mayne acknowledges as the most compelling of stories.

Without question, one of the most arresting aspects of Luke 15:11-32 is the image in verse 20 of the father actually looking, searching for his lost son to return, and then, upon spotting him, running to greet his son and throwing his arms around him and kissing him in an unmistakable gesture of reconciliation. This is a lasting image, arguably the defining image, along with the crucifixion, underlying the theology that God is love. Hume has this image in mind when he writes, ". . . we would not be seeking God, unless he were first seeking us."[73] Hume delights in telling the story of once having a letter from a woman who wrote that a man who later became a prominent Christian said that his idea of God was "revolutionised" when, as a young boy, he was taken to visit a woman who pointed out to him a text on the wall which read: "Thou, God, seest me." The woman said to the boy: "You see those words? They do not mean that God is always watching you to see what you are doing wrong. They mean that he loves you so much that he cannot take his eyes off you."[74] In his own words,

Hume claims: "The Father is in search of us always. . ." [75] Commenting on verse 20 specifically, he asks: "Can anything be more moving, more consoling, than that little scene, which speaks so eloquently of the way God sees and understands each one of us?"[76] Hume believes passionately that because of God's limitless love for us, true religion, ". . . carries always within itself the seeds of renewal and fresh hope. Genuine religious experience leads eventually to reconciliation and new life."[77] This is the message of Luke 15:11-32.

Commentators agree that a very key point in the parable is verse 17, when the prodigal comes to himself. And there is general agreement that the father's gracious welcome offered to the prodigal upon his return is the central focus of the story, around which all other important aspects of the parable revolve. Volf argues that the most significant aspect of the story, however, is that the father, though he does allow the prodigal to depart physically, never lets go of the relationship between them. In Volf's view: "The eyes that searched for and finally caught sight of the son in 'the distance' (v. 20) tell of a heart that was with the son in the 'distant country' (v. 13)."[78] Though far from home in a physical sense, the young son remained in the father's heart.[79] Mayne echoes Volf's sentiments, as God the Father is "wholly Love," and that, ". . . to be reconciled to God is to be caught up into 'a love that will not let us go.'"[80]

The parable of the Prodigal Son is, as has been noted earlier, arguably the most compelling story in the Bible in communicating that God's response to humanity is grace-filled. When students of the Bible think, 'God is love', Luke 15:11-32 is likely, consciously or subconsciously, to be behind that theological presupposition. Prather reminds readers: "God isn't interested in your catalogue of mistakes. God wants you to remember your perfection this instant."[81] Perfection here cannot connote sinlessness or moral perfection. It does imply, however, completeness, the capacity to experience forgiveness and reconciliation. Prather asserts: "God doesn't dwell on our errors."[82] Yet again Prather's comments conjure up images from Luke 15:11-32 when he writes that God is, ". . . the welcome we cannot wear out."[83]

In speaking of the unconditional love of God, Mayne believes, ". . . it is when we begin to grasp what it means to be so loved that we are set free to repent, and to receive that forgiveness."[84] For Mayne, compassion and mercy are the two words which are the, ". . . starting-point for all our thinking about the nature of God and against which all other claims to the truth and insight must be tested."[85] With Luke 15:11-32 squarely in mind, Mayne claims that God, ". . . knows me infinitely better than I know myself, and graciously welcomes me home, not in spite of what I have been but because of what I am. 'Graciously': the action of grace. 'Home': the place where I can shed all pretense, where 'everything is known and yet forgiven.'"[86]

An aspect of the father's unconditional love is his compassion. Verse 20 makes clear that the father is not only excited to see his returning son, but that he is filled with compassion for his precious child. Keen writes persuasively that compassion is to be at the very center of an authentically spiritual life. He holds that in the spiritual journey, ". . . the compass unfailingly points toward compassion."[87] He goes so far as to write: "Inscribe this single word on your heart—'compassion.' Whenever you are confused, keep heading in the direction that leads toward deepening your love and care for all living beings including yourself, and you will never stray far from the path to fulfillment."[88]

The image of the father in the parable contributes to sentiments such as Prather expresses when he writes: "The true need—as it has always been—is merely to love, to accept, to be quick to help, to be slow to judge."[89] O'Donohue concurs with the belief that compassion is to be at the center of the spiritual life. In a very practical sense, he suggests regarding personal relationships: "When you meet someone with a difficult or abrasive personality, you may move away from him or her. If you begin to wonder what made a person become like that, you may be more open to the hidden story that has shaped this awkward presence. Wonder can often be the key to compassion."[90]

Crucially, Volf notes regarding the reconciliation between the prodigal and his father that: "For the embrace to be complete—for the celebration to begin—a confession of wrongdoing had to be made."[91] Verse 21 makes clear the fact that the prodigal does confess his sin. He expresses his deep remorse in admitting that he is no longer worthy to be his father's son. Volf's cautionary note regarding confession is a reminder that what is offered in Luke 15:11-32 is not 'cheap grace'. The prodigal is forgiven, unconditionally, but in order to fully receive and embrace such grace, it is necessary for him to come to the father in humility, acknowledging his need for forgiveness and mercy. Battle writes: "Love, as we learn to embrace it, leads us toward the banquet of reconciliation."[92] A part of being able to embrace love is learning to be honest with ourselves, and coming to terms with the message that we are beloved as we are, in our full humanness, through the grace of God.

In our own efforts toward reconciliation with sisters and brothers in the human family, we are to learn from the father in Luke 15:11-32 to pattern our efforts after his model of compassion and grace-filled love. In his study of Desmond Tutu's heroic work toward reconciliation in South Africa and elsewhere, Battle observes that consistently, Tutu's voice carries a conciliatory tone even as he attacks racist ideology.[93]

The figure of the father in Luke 15:11-32 is, indeed, the embodiment of grace. He prefigures the grace that Jesus himself will offer once and for all on the cross. The father in the parable of the Prodigal Son is an essential figure in the development of a biblically-based theology of grace. Paul F. M. Zahl argues that grace is the "overarching paradigm" of the New Testament.[94] Zahl defines grace as "one-way love," and asserts that it is the "heart of Christianity."[95] Indeed, for Zahl this one-way love, ". . . is what makes Christianity Christian."[96] In the father of Luke 15:11-32, we see the embodiment of what Zahl terms God's one-way love. Bryan P. Stone's theology of ministry agrees with Zahl's focus on grace as being the absolute heart of Christian faith and practice. In his very fine book on the theology of ministry, titled *Compassionate Ministry: Theological Foundations*, Stone asserts: "Ministry, in sum, has a kind of threefold character: it is a response to grace, it is a participation in grace, and it is an offer of grace."[97]

Williams observes that Jesus himself knew the grace of God, which informed his own joy, and thus his passionate invitation to humanity to embrace God's forgiveness and love. Williams writes of Jesus: "The joy which is his can only be the awareness of being held absolutely in the gaze of the Father, receiving moment by moment the completeness of his love."[98] Hume argues that in the parable of the Prodigal Son Jesus is revealing in a definitive way what God is like, and that Jesus is teaching that this image of a loving, forgiving God, ". . . has to be the thought and inspiration of our lives. We have got to allow the thought of his love to become a deep conviction."[99] Referring specifically to the father's kissing his desperate, humiliated young son upon his return, Hume states: "You get tears in your eyes when you think of that. The father had been watching out, hoping against hope that he would see his son coming home."[100] In Hume's view: "The greatest grace which God can give is the knowledge that he loves each one of us more than any lover ever loved his, or her, beloved. To realize that, and to allow it to sink deep into our minds and hearts, can change our lives completely."[101]

Tutu both humbly and poignantly acknowledges that, in the end, he has only one sermon, ". . . that God loves us freely as an act of grace, that we do not have to impress God in order for God to love us as a reward."[102] Similarly, Hume asserts, ". . . few thoughts are more exhilarating than the realisation that 'God is love' and that he has for each person an intensity of love which no human experience of love can match."[103] The image of the father in Luke 15:11-32 is intended to communicate the intensity of God's love for us. O'Donohue observes that: "Something about Jesus' presence offered people a new life. Religion has often forgotten this and fashioned an image of God which only brings fear and guilt on us."[104] The parable is offered to show that God is love and that, rather than harshness, God is to be understood as merciful, hungry to forgive, and to offer reconciliation.

Mayne asserts that the two cardinal lessons in all of life are, ". . . how to love and how to trust."[105] Luke 15:11-32 addresses these two lessons as directly and as compellingly as any other passage in the Bible. We learn from the father how to love, and we learn that the Father (God) can be trusted to love us in our full humanity and sinfulness. Prather writes tellingly: "God speaks to us in a thousand voices, each with the same clear message: 'I love you. Please trust me on this one.'"[106]

In an unforgettably searching phrase, Dillard writes in *Teaching a Stone to Talk*: "So once in Israel love came to us incarnate, stood in the doorway between two worlds, and we were all afraid."[107] In the parable of the Prodigal Son, Jesus teaches his hearers the source of his love—the Father.

In comparison to his overtly sinful younger brother, the elder son in the parable considers himself to be righteous, the 'good child'. In the historical context in which the parable was first told, the elder child represents those Pharisees and scribes who resented Jesus' inclusion of those who, from the perspective of the

Pharisees and scribes, were unrighteous. The Pharisees and scribes who are critical of Jesus' more inclusive orientation considered themselves to be the faithful followers of God. Dillard reminds her readers that faith is not merely assenting intellectually to a series of doctrinal propositions but is instead, "...living in conscious and rededicated relationship to God."[108] In offering the parable to his harsh critics, Jesus is extending to them an invitation to turn their hearts and to rejoice with those who are turning to him to renew their faith. In other words, Jesus invites the Pharisees and scribes to celebrate with those who are being 'found', and in the process be renewed in their own relationships with God.

Volf points out that, unlike the father, the older brother did not keep his younger sibling in his heart while he was in the foreign country.[109] Volf notes that the older brother judges his younger brother employing moral categories to do so. In so doing the elder brother sees himself as being 'good', while the prodigal is 'bad'. The father, however, although acutely aware of the moral implications of the prodigal's behavior, sees his younger son in relational categories. In Volf's view, to the father the younger son is not 'bad', but 'lost'. The father in the parable teaches us that with God: "Relationship is prior to moral rules; moral performance may do something to the relationship, but relationship is not grounded in moral performance."[110]

The elder son's judgmentalism toward his younger sibling is evidenced in his refusal to recognize the prodigal as his brother. In his judgmentalism, the elder son seeks to separate himself from his brother. Prather reminds his readers that a foundation of the spiritual life is to recognize that as children of God we are, indeed, sisters and brothers.[111] In a similar vein, Keen writes: "What we call 'the spiritual life' and 'the spiritual quest' are simply ways we discover to transcend our delusions of our own separateness, superiority, or inferiority and gradually feel our identity with our fellow human beings and compassion for them"[112] Keen further asserts: "The human future depends on whether we can learn we are kinfolk, and be kind to one another."[113] In his book on the reconciliation theology of Tutu, Battle recalls Tutu's belief that reconciliation is, "...a deeply personal affair among equals. It can only happen between persons of shared identity."[114] In the parable, Jesus is reminding his critics that all of God's children ultimately share an identity as His equally beloved children.

Having said all of this, siblings can, of course, be very different! A shared identity as children of God does not connote exact sameness. Williams cautions along these lines: "Recognizing the other as other without the immediate impulse to make them the same involves recognizing the incompleteness of the world I think I can manage so well, but which has more depth of reality. And that must be to move closer to God."[115] As human beings move closer to God, to use Williams' term, we learn how better to love and accept our human siblings.

In addressing the subject of judgmentalism, Tutu wisely observes: "One of the lessons I have learned as I have grown older is that we should be a great deal more modest in claims we make about our prowess and our various capacities. Even more importantly, we should be generous in our judgments of others, for we can never really know all there is to know about another."[116] Similarly, and directly in line with Luke 15:11-32, Mayne states: "None of us dare judge the life of another: that is God's prerogative, and his judgement is matched by his mercy."[117]

One of the crucial lessons the elder son teaches in the parable is that rather than viewing others with judgment and self-righteousness, the more spiritually healthy attitude is thanksgiving for God's love and mercy toward us. Keen urges an orientation toward thankfulness in saying: "...the more you become a connoisseur of gratitude, the less you are the victim of resentment, depression, and despair."[118] He notes: "Gratitude will act as an elixir that will gradually dissolve the hard shell of your ego—your need to possess and control—and transform you into a generous being."[119] A humble orientation toward gratitude produces, "...true spiritual alchemy, [and] makes us magnanimous—large souled."[120] Keen also notes: "To develop the widest compassion, I must ultimately know that *nothing human is alien to me.* I am monster and saint, murderer and healer, contaminated and pure."[121] This lesson is contained powerfully in the figure of the elder son, who is in no position to stand in judgment of his younger sibling.

Echoing Keen's sentiments regarding thankfulness, Mayne writes that it is a way of being, a mindset that is, "...trusting rather than anxious, grateful rather than grudging, compassionate rather than judgmental, and outgoing rather than selfish."[122] The Pharisees and scribes to whom Jesus addresses the parable would be wise to turn their hearts toward a more gratitude-centered orientation. Similarly to his sentiments expressed in *A Year Lost and Found,* in *Pray, Love, Remember* Mayne writes that no one can ever really understand the heart of another person, and that, "...none of us dare pass judgement on anyone else's life or death. That is God's prerogative, for he alone perfectly understands, and his judgement is always more than matched by his mercy."[123]

The elder brother's reaction to the prodigal's return is the mirror opposite of that of the father. The forgiveness and reconciliation offered by the father to the prodigal are met by absolute resistance from the older sibling, whose hardness of heart is abundantly clear. The father urges his eldest son to come in to the celebration and rejoice in his younger brother's return, but, sadly, the invitation is, at least initially, rejected. As verse 32 comes to an end, the reader is left to ponder whether the elder son ever relented, forgave his younger sibling, and welcomed his brother home.

In his contribution to *The Sunflower,* Tutu writes poignantly: "Without forgiveness, there is no future."[124] Indeed, one of Tutu's major works is titled, *No Future Without Forgiveness.* In addressing his critics directly with the parable of the Prodigal Son, Jesus is urging them to soften their hostility toward the 'unrighteous', and to rejoice in their repentance, rather than refusing to offer their own forgiveness to their returning sisters and brothers. The elder son considers his younger sibling unworthy of his father's gracious reception, seeing as how he, the elder, though he has not left home, has never been offered even a smaller, more modest celebration in his own honor. Battle writes that: "To practice reconciliation is to develop the habit of seeing beyond the natural instinct of retaliation."[125] Similarly, Mayne observes that whether on a global scale, or between two people, there are always two possible responses to hurt, "...to pass it on, in the form of negative retaliation, an upping of the stakes; or to 'absorb' it, not passively but with a deliberate breaking of the chain."[126]

The elder son's jealousy is readily apparent in verses 29-30. Another way to frame his reaction to the prodigal's return is hurt, his feeling that his goodness, his apparent faithfulness has been taken for granted. Prather encourages his readers: "Practice having no ego, and you will be free."[127] It is difficult to imagine any more profound, or more practical spiritual guidance regarding issues of jealousy or of judgmentalism. In the parable, the father assures the elder brother that he is just as precious, just as loved as is his younger brother. To celebrate the prodigal's homecoming in no way relegates his older brother to a secondary status. Jesus is trying to reassure his critics that repentant sinners in no way threaten or displace those who have been 'at home' all along. Prather also counsels: "Quickly forgive another his mistakes. Do not leave your mind at war."[128] The elder brother's anger is readily apparent when he refuses to acknowledge the prodigal as being his sibling. The father's gracious invitation to his elder son is for him to be at peace—with his brother, with the father, and, ultimately, to be at peace with himself, with who he is, and where he fits in the family structure.

As was stated earlier, verses 25-32 are not an appendage to the main body of the parable, as a handful of scholars have suggested. Indeed, by the end of the story the focus has shifted from the prodigal to his elder brother. Battle goes so far as to say: "The parable becomes a diptych in which the elder son ultimately becomes the focus of the parable, which is more concerned with the fault of the elder son than that of the younger son."[129] The father's invitation to the elder son to join in the celebration of the prodigal's homecoming is, in Battle's view, representative of the fact that, "...reunion is God's ultimate gift and hope for us."[130]

As the parable closes, the father counters angry and divisive language with positive images of reconciliation and unity, summoning the elder son to, in Donahue's term, "...a feast of life."[131] The Pharisees and scribes of Luke 15:2 are being summoned by Jesus to join the feast when precious children of God return home. Hendrickx claims that, in its literary context, Luke uses the parable to foster an ecclesial attitude, "...by which the community searches for the lost, is prepared for reconciliation, and integrates all in the house of the Father."[132] Without question, Luke envisions the parable as carrying with it a "missionary dimension."[133]

In summarizing the parable's overarching function in Luke's gospel, Barton writes that Luke's message to his readers is that: "It is a time not for dividing into parties antagonistic to one another, but for uniting in a new kind of solidarity that is grounded on the grace of God and sustained by ongoing practices of repentance, forgiveness and reconciliation."[134] In summarizing the parable's potential pastoral application nearly 2,000 years after it was first told, Hume wisely counsels: "I think that whenever one is depressed about life, or over-whelmed by guilt feelings, if ever one is overcome by a sense of one's own in-adequacy, or whenever going through difficult periods, it is good just to go and read quietly and prayerfully Luke chapter 15. It is a marvelous revelation of what we mean to God revealed by Our Lord himself, the highest authority."[135]

Notes

1. Simon Wiesenthal, *The Sunflower: On the Possibilities and Limits of Forgiveness.* Revised and Expanded Edition (New York: Schocken Books, 1969), 169.
2. Michael Mayne, *The Enduring Melody* (London: Darton, Longman and Todd, Ltd., 2006), 119.
3. Ibid., 114.
4. Basil Hume, *The Mystery of the Incarnation* (London: Darton, Longman and Todd, Ltd., 1999), 72.
5. Miroslav Volf, *Exclusion and Embrace: A Theological Exploration of Identity, Otherness, and Reconciliation* (Nashville: Abingdon Press, 1996), 156.
6. Ibid.
7. W. Mark Richardson, "Introduction." *Anglican Theological Review* 89 (Spring 2007): 191.
8. Pheme Perkins, *Hearing the Parables of Jesus* (New York: Paulist Press, 1981), 61.
9. Michael Battle, *Practicing Reconciliation in a Violent World* (Harrisburg, PA: Morehouse Publishing, 2005), 78.
10. Michael Battle, *Reconciliation: The Ubuntu Theology of Desmond Tutu* (Cleveland: The Pilgrim Press, 1997), 67.
11. Ibid., 68.
12. Titus Presler, "Listening Toward Reconciliation: A Conversation Initiative in To-day's Anglican Alienations." *Anglican Theological Review* 89 (Spring 2007): 252.
13. Ann Belford Ulanov, "Practicing Reconciliation: Love and Work." *Anglican Theological Review* 89 (Spring 2007): 246.
14. Johnson, 241.
15. Bernard Brandon Scott, *Hear Then the Parable: A Commentary on the Parables of Jesus* (Minneapolis: Fortress Press, 1989), 125.
16. David Bryan Hoopes, "From the Superior." *Holy Cross: Newsletter of the Order of the Holy Cross* 26 (Summer 2005): 2.
17. Battle, *Practicing Reconciliation*, 64.
18. Desmond Mpilo Tutu, *No Future Without Forgiveness* (New York: Image Books, 1999), 287.
19. Ibid., 270.
20. Mayne, *Learning to Dance*, 167.
21. Battle, *Practicing Reconciliation*, 48.
22. Richardson, 191.
23. Rowan Williams, *The Truce of God* (Grand Rapids: William B. Eerdmans Publishing Company, 2005), 57.

24. John R. Claypool, *Tracks of a Fellow Struggler: Living and Growing Through Grief.* Revised Edition (New Orleans: Insight Press, 1995), 70.
25. Battle, *Practicing Reconciliation,* 51.
26. Ibid.
27. John O'Donohue, *Anam Cara: A Book of Celtic Wisdom* (New York: Cliff Street Books, 1997), xvii.
28. Culpepper, 304.
29. Annie Dillard, *An American Childhood* (New York: HarperPerennial, 1987), 248.
30. Tutu, 175.
31. Volf, 158.
32. Sam Keen, *Fire in the Belly: On Being a Man* (New York: Bantam Books, 1991), 226.
33. Ibid.
34. Ibid., 151.
35. Basil Hume, *The Mystery of Love* (London: Darton, Longman and Todd, Ltd., 2000), 23.
36. Frederick Buechner, *Telling Secrets* (New York: HarperCollins, 1991), 2.
37. Ibid., 92.
38. Ibid.
39. Hume, *The Mystery of the Incarnation*, 71.
40. Ibid.
41. Ibid., 82.
42. Ibid. 70.
43. Ibid.
44. Mayne, *The Enduring Melody*, 40.
45. Ibid.
46. Ibid., 128.
47. Rick Mathis, *The Christ-Centered Heart: Peaceful Living in Difficult Times* (Liguori, MO: Liguori/Triumph, 1999), 122.
48. Buechner, *Telling Secrets*, 74.
49. Hugh Prather, *The Quiet Answer* (New York: Doubleday, 1982), 139.
50. O'Donohue, *Anam Cara*, 183.
51. Michael Mayne, *A Year Lost and Found* (London: Darton, Longman and Todd, Ltd., 1987), 71.
52. Frederick Buechner, *The Sacred Journey* (New York: HarperSanFrancisco, 1982), 56.
53. John O'Donohue, *Eternal Echoes: Exploring Our Yearning to Belong* (New York: Cliff Street Books, 1999), 172.
54. Ibid.
55. Wiesenthal, 182.
56. Ibid., 169.
57. Battle, *Reconciliation*, 44.
58. Williams, *The Truce of God,* 96.
59. Ibid., 23.
60. Hume, *The Mystery of the Incarnation,* 96.
61. Ibid.
62. Hume, *The Mystery of Love,* 94.
63. Hume, *The Mystery of the Incarnation,* 155.
64. Wiesenthal, 169.

65. Michael Mayne, *Pray, Love, Remember* (London: Darton, Longman and Todd, Ltd., 1998), 122.
66. Michael Mayne, *This Sunrise of Wonder: Letters to my grandchildren* (London: Fount, 1995), 258.
67. Hume, *The Mystery of Love*, 23.
68. Sam Keen, *Hymns To An Unknown God: Awakening the Spirit in Everyday Life* (New York: Bantam Books, 1994), 22.
69. Ibid., 229.
70. Battle, *Practicing Reconciliation*, 39.
71. Ibid., 5.
72. Mayne, *This Sunrise of Wonder*, 248.
73. Hume, *The Mystery of Love*, 6.
74. Hume, *The Mystery of the Incarnation*, 91.
75. Ibid., 73.
76. Ibid.
77. Ibid., 56.
78. Volf, 159.
79. Ibid.
80. Mayne, *A Year Lost and Found*, 53.
81. Hugh Prather, *Spiritual Notes to Myself: Essential Wisdom for the 21st Century* (New York: MJF Books, 1998), 94.
82. Ibid., 138.
83. Ibid., 86.
84. Mayne, *Learning to Dance*, 169.
85. Mayne, *The Enduring Melody*, 205.
86. Ibid., 33.
87. Keen, *Hymns To An Unknown God*, 59.
88. Ibid.
89. Hugh Prather, *How to Live in the World and Still Be Happy* (York Beach, ME: Conari Press, 2002), 213.
90. O'Donohue, *Eternal Echoes*, 197.
91. Volf, 160.
92. Battle, *Practicing Reconciliation*, 40.
93. Battle, *Reconciliation*, xiii.
94. Paul F. M. Zahl, *Grace In Practice: A Theology of Everyday Life* (Grand Rapids: William B. Eerdmans Publishing Company, 2007), 39.
95. Ibid., ix.
96. Ibid.
97. Bryan P. Stone, *Compassionate Ministry: Theological Foundations* (Maryknoll, NY: Orbis Books, 1996), 43.
98. Rowan Williams, *Christ on Trial: How the Gospel Unsettles Our Judgement* (Grand Rapids: William B. Eerdmans Publishing Company, 2000), 90.
99. Hume, *The Mystery of Love*, 86.
100. Ibid.
101. Ibid., 92.
102. Tutu, 185.
103. Hume, *The Mystery of the Incarnation*, 54.
104. O'Donohue, *Eternal Echoes*, 165.
105. Mayne, *Pray, Love, Remember*, 26.

106. Prather, *Spiritual Notes,* 7.
107. Annie Dillard, *Teaching a Stone to Talk: Expeditions and Encounters* (New York: Harper & Row, Publishers, 1982), 139.
108. Annie Dillard, *For The Time Being* (New York: Vintage Books, 1999), 146.
109. Volf, 161.
110. Ibid., 164.
111. Prather, *Spiritual Notes*, 103.
112. Keen, *Hymns*, 36.
113. Ibid., 291.
114. Battle, *Reconciliation*, 101.
115. Williams, *Christ on Trial*, 62.
116. Tutu, 169.
117. Mayne, *A Year Lost and Found,* 71.
118. Keen, *Hymns,* 275.
119. Ibid.
120. Ibid.
121. Ibid., 164.
122. Mayne, *This Sunrise of Wonder*, 296.
123. Mayne, *Pray, Love, Remember*, 58.
124. Wiesenthal, 268.
125. Battle, *Practicing Reconciliation,* 70.
126. Mayne, *Learning to Dance*, 173.
127. Prather, *Spiritual Notes*, 112.
128. Prather, *The Quiet Answer*, 88.
129. Battle, *Practicing Reconciliation*, 34.
130. Ibid., 46.
131. Donahue, 157.
132. Hendrickx, 166.
133. Ibid.
134. Barton, 214.
135. Hume, *The Mystery of Love*, 85.

Postscript

I can remember with great clarity a particular Saturday evening during my high school years. While returning home from a night out, I made a youthful mistake while driving the family car. No one was hurt, and the accident was by no means catastrophic or tragic in any sense. Nonetheless, I knew that the damage to the left side of the car was significant and would cost hundreds of dollars to repair, if indeed it could be repaired. Though unhurt, I was deeply embarrassed to have caused such damage to the family car when I was trying to be so careful. I never went to sleep that night, tossing and turning constantly as I pondered how I would tell my parents what had happened and what their response might be.

The next morning, before church, I told my father that I had something to show him and that he needed to come outside. Once outside, I confessed to him what had happened, that no one else was involved, no one was hurt, but that I had obviously torn up the left side of the family's main vehicle. All night long I had worried about how he would react to my foolish, youthful, expensive mistake. Though hardly tragic, I had, I was sure, disappointed him and myself. In my mind, my father had every right to be furious with me.

To his credit, and to my amazement, he was not angry. I can remember him saying with absolute calmness: "It's just metal. We'll get it fixed." He then told me that he appreciated my being honest with him about what I had done, to which I responded in a nervously joking way: "Well, it's not like I can hide it." My father's response to me was: "You can always be honest with me. You're my boy, and I'll always love you."

Luke 15:11-32

Bibliography

Augustine. *Confessions*. Tr. with an Introduction by R. S. Pine-Coffin. New York:Penguin Books, 1961.

Aus, David Roger. "Luke 15:11-32 and R. Eliezer Ben Hyrcanus's Rise to Fame." *Journal of Biblical Literature* 104 (1985): 443-69.

Austin, Michael R. "The Hypocritical Son." *The Evangelical Quarterly* 57 (October 1985): 307-15.

Bailey, Kenneth E. *The Cross and the Prodigal: Luke 15 Through the Eyes of Middle Eastern Peasants*. Second Edition. Downers Grove, IL: InterVarsity Press, 2005.

Barclay, William. *The Gospel of Luke*. The New Daily Study Bible. Louisville: Westminster John Knox Press, 2001.

——. *The Parables of Jesus*. Louisville: Westminster John Knox Press, 1970.

Barton, Stephen C. "Parables on God's Love and Forgiveness (Luke 15:1-32)." In *The Challenge of Jesus' Parables*. McMaster New Testament Studies. Richard N. Longenecker, Editor. Grand Rapids: William B. Eerdmans Publishing Company, 2000: 199-216.

Battle, Michael. *Practicing Reconciliation in a Violent World*. Harrisburg, PA: More-house Publishing, 2005.

——. *Reconciliation: The Ubuntu Theology of Desmond Tutu*. Cleveland, OH: The Pilgrim Press, 1997.

Bock, Darrell L. *Luke*. Volume 2: 9:51-24:53. Baker Exegetical Commentary on the New Testament. Grand Rapids: Baker Books, 1996.

——. *The NIV Application Bible: Luke*. Grand Rapids: Zondervan Publishing House, 1996.

Book of Common Prayer, The. New York: Church Hymnal Corporation, 1979.

Borsch, Frederick Houk. *Many Things in Parables: Extravagant Stories of New Community*. Philadelphia: Fortress Press, 1988.

Boucher, Madeleine I. *The Parables*. New Testament Message. A Biblical-Theological Commentary. Wilfrid Harrington and Donald Senior Editors. Wilmington, DE: Michael Glazier, Inc., 1981.

Bowie, Walter Russell. *The Compassionate Christ: Reflections from the Gospel of Luke.* Nashville: Abingdon Press, 1965.

Brown, Robert R. *Alive Again.* New York: Morehouse-Barlow Co., 1964.

Brunner, Emil. *Sowing and Reaping: The Parables of Jesus.* Tr. Thomas Wieser. Richmond: John Knox Press, 1946.

Buechner, Frederick. *Now and Then.* New York: HarperSanFrancisco, 1983.

——. *The Sacred Journey.* New York: HarperSanFrancisco, 1982.

——. *Telling Secrets.* New York: HarperCollins, 1991.

Bultmann, Rudolf K. *The History of the Synoptic Tradition.* Revised Edition. Tr. John Marsh. New York: Harper & Row, 1963.

Caird, George B. *The Gospel of Luke.* The Pelican Gospel Commentaries. Baltimore: Penguin Books, 1963.

Capon, Robert Farrar. *The Parables of Grace.* Grand Rapids: William B. Eerdmans Publishing Company, 1988.

Claypool, John R. *Tracks of a Fellow Struggler: Living and Growing Through Grief.* Revised Edition. New Orleans: Insight Press, 1995.

Compton, J. E. "The Prodigal's Brother." *Expository Times* Volume 42 (1931): 287.

Corlett, Tom. "This Brother of Yours." *Expository Times* Volume 100 (March 1989): 216.

Craddock, Fred B. "Luke." In *Harper's Bible Commentary.* James L. Mays, General Editor. San Francisco: Harper & Row Publishers, 1988.

——. *Luke.* Interpretation: A Bible Commentary for Teaching and Preaching. Louisville: John Knox Press, 1990.

Crawford, R. G. "A Parable of the Atonement." *The Evangelical Quarterly* Volume 50 (January-March 1978): 2-7.

Crossan, John Dominic, Editor. *Semeia 9: Polyvalent Narration.* Missoula, MT: Scholars Press, 1977.

Culpepper, R. Alan. "The Gospel of Luke." *The New Interpreter's Bible,* Volume IX. Nashville: Abingdon, 1995.

Danker, Frederick W. *Jesus and the New Age: A Commentary on St. Luke's Gospel.* Philadelphia: Fortress Press, 1988.

Derrett, J. Duncan M. "Law in the New Testament: The Parable of the Prodigal Son." *New Testament Studies* Volume 14 (October 1967): 56-74.

Dillard, Annie. *An American Childhood.* New York: HarperPerennial, 1987.

——. *For The Time Being.* New York: Vintage Books, 1999.

——. *Teaching a Stone to Talk: Expeditions and Encounters.* New York: Harper & Row, Publishers, 1982.

Donahue, John R. *The Gospel in Parable: Metaphor, Narrative, and Theology in the Synoptic Gospels.* Philadelphia: Fortress Press, 1988.

Drury, John. *The Gospel of Luke: A Commentary on the New Testament in Modern English.* The J. B. Phillips' Commentaries. New York: Macmillan Publishing Co., Inc., 1973.

Easton, Burton Scott. *The Gospel According to St. Luke: A Critical and Exegetical Commentary.* New York: Charles Scribner's Sons, 1926.

Etchells, Ruth. *A Reading of the Parables of Jesus*. London: Darton, Longman and Todd, Ltd., 1988.

Evans, C. F. *Saint Luke*. TPI New Testament Commentaries. Philadelphia: Trinity Press International, 1990.

Evans, Craig A. *Luke*. The International Biblical Commentary. Peabody, MA: Hendrickson Publishers, Inc., 1990.

Faley, Roland J. "There Once Was a Man Who Had Two Sons..." *The Bible Today* Volume 18 (1965): 1181-86.

Fisher, Neal F. *The Parables of Jesus: Glimpses of God's Reign*. New York: Crossroad, 1990.

Fitzmyer, Joseph A. *The Gospel According to Luke X-XXIV*. The Anchor Bible. New York: Doubleday, 1985.

Geldenhuys, Norval. *Commentary on the Gospel of Luke*. The New International Commentary on the New Testament. Grand Rapids: William B. Eerdmans Green, Joel B. *The Gospel of Luke*. Grand Rapids: William B. Eerdmans Publishing Company, 1997.

Harrington, Wilfrid. "The Prodigal Son." *Furrow* Volume 25 (August 1974): 432-7.

Hendrickx, Herman. *The Parables of Jesus*. San Francisco: Harper & Row, Publishers, 1986.

Hoopes, David Bryan. "From The Superior." *Holy Cross: Newsletter of the Order of the Holy Cross* Volume 26 (Summer 2005): 2-4.

Hultgren, Arland J. *The Parables of Jesus: A Commentary*. The Bible In Its World. David Noel Freeman, General Editor. Grand Rapids: William B. Eerdmans Publishing Company, 2000.

Hume, Basil. *The Mystery of the Incarnation*. London: Darton, Longman and Todd, Ltd., 1999.

——. *The Mystery of Love*. London: Darton, Longman and Todd, Ltd., 2000.

Hunter, Archibald M. *Interpreting the Parables*. Philadelphia: Westminster Press, 1960.

Jeremias, Joachim. *New Testament Theology: The Proclamation of Jesus*. Tr. John Bowden. New York: Charles Scribner's Sons, 1971.

——. *Rediscovering the Parables*. New York: Charles Scribner's Sons, 1966.

Johnson, Luke Timothy. *The Gospel of Luke*. Sacra Pagina Series, Volume 3. Collegeville, MN: The Liturgical Press, 1991.

Kalas, J. Ellsworth. *The Parables of Jesus*. Nashville: Abingdon Press, 1997.

Keen, Sam. *Fire in the Belly: On Being a Man*. New York: Bantam Books, 1991.

——. *Hymns To An Unknown God: Awakening the Spirit in Everyday Life*. New York: Bantam Books, 1994.

Kendall, R. T. *The Complete Guide to the Parables: Understanding and Applying the Stories of Jesus*. Grand Rapids: Chosen Books, 2004.

La Verdiere, Eugene. *Luke*. New Testament Message, Wilfrid Harrington and Donald Senior, Editors. Wilmington, DE: Michael Glazier, Inc., 1980.

Leaney, A. R. C. *The Gospel According to St. Luke.* Harper's New Testament Commentaries. Henry Chadwick, General Editor. New York: Harper & Brothers Publishers, 1958.

Lenski, R. C. H. *Commentary on the New Testament: The Interpretation of St. Luke's Gospel.* Hendrickson Publishers, Inc., Edition. Second Printing, 2001 (Original Copyright 1946, The Wartburg Press).

Lieu, Judith. *The Gospel of Luke.* Epworth Commentaries. Ivor H. Jones, General Editor. Peterborough: Epworth Press, 1997.

Marshall, I. Howard. *The Gospel of Luke: A Commentary on the Greek Text.* The New International Greek Testament Commentary. Grand Rapids: Paternoster Press, 1978.

Mathis, Rick. *The Christ-Centered Heart: Peaceful Living in Difficult Times.* Liguori, MO: Liguori/Triumph, 1999.

Mayne, Michael. *The Enduring Melody.* London: Darton, Longman and Todd, Ltd., 2006.

——. *Learning to Dance.* London: Darton, Longman and Todd, Ltd., 2001.

——. *Pray, Love, Remember.* London: Darton, Longman and Todd, Ltd., 1998.

——. *This Sunrise of Wonder: Letters to my grandchildren.* London: Fount, 1995.

——. *A Year Lost and Found.* London: Darton, Longman and Todd, Ltd., 1987.

Moorman, John R. H. *The Path to Glory: Studies in the Gospel According to St. Luke.* London: SPCK and Seabury Press, 1960.

Morgan, G. Campbell. *The Gospel According to Luke.* Grand Rapids: Fleming H. Revell, 1931.

Morris, Leon. *The Gospel According to St. Luke.* The Tyndale New Testament Commentaries. Grand Rapids: Eerdmans, 1974.

Nickle, Keith F. *Preaching the Gospel of Luke: Proclaiming God's Royal Rule.* Louisville: Westminster John Knox Press, 2000.

Nolland, John. *Word Biblical Commentary: Luke 9:21-18:34.* Volume 35B. Waco, TX: Word Incorporated, 1993.

Nouwen, Henri J. M. *The Return of the Prodigal Son: A Story of Homecoming.* New York: Doubleday, 1992.

O'Donohue, John. *Anam Cara: A Book of Celtic Wisdom.* New York: Cliff Street Books, 1997.

——. *Eternal Echoes: Exploring Our Yearning to Belong.* New York: Cliff Street Books, 1997.

O'Rourke, John J. "Some Notes on Luke 15:11-32." *New Testament Studies* Volume 18 (July 1972): 431-3.

Osborn, Robert T. "The Father and His Two Sons: A Parable of Liberation." *Dialog* Volume 19 (Summer 1980): 204-9.

Perkins, Pheme. *Hearing the Parables of Jesus.* New York: Paulist Press, 1981.

Plummer, Alfred. *A Critical and Exegetical Commentary on The Gospel According To St. Luke.* The International Critical Commentary. Fifth Edition. Edinburgh: T & T Clark, 1896.

Prather, Hugh. *How to Live in the World and Still Be Happy.* York Beach, ME: Conari Press, 2002.

——. *The Quiet Answer.* New York: Doubleday, 1982.

——. *Spiritual Notes to Myself: Essential Wisdom for the 21st Century* New York: MJF Books, 1998.

Presler, Titus. "Listening Toward Reconciliation: A Conversation Initiative in Today's Anglican Alienations." *Anglican Theological Review* 89 (Spring 2007): 247-66.

Price, James L. "Luke 15:11-32." *Interpretation* Volume 31 (January 1977): 64-9.

Richardson, W. Mark. "Introduction." *Anglican Theological Review* 89 (Spring 2007): 191-4.

Rickards, Raymond R. "Some Points to Consider in Translating The Parable of the Prodigal Son (Luke 15:11-32)." *The Bible Translator* Volume 31 (April 1980): 243-5.

Ringe, Sharon H. *Luke.* Westminster Bible Companion. Louisville: Westminster John Knox Press, 1995.

Sanders, E. P. *Jesus and Judaism.* Philadelphia: Fortress Press, 1985.

Sanders, Jack T. "Tradition and Redaction in Luke 15:11-32." *New Testament Studies* Volume 15 (July 1969): 433-8.

Schweizer, Eduard. *The Good News According to Luke.* Tr. David E. Green. Atlanta: John Knox Press, 1984.

Scott, Bernard Brandon. *Hear Then the Parable: A Commentary on the Parables of Jesus.* Minneapolis: Fortress Press, 1989.

Stein, Robert H. *Luke.* The New American Commentary, Volume 24. Nashville: Broadman Press, 2004.

Stickler, H. E. "The Prodigal's Brother." *Expository Times* Volume 42 (1930): 45-46.

Stone, Bryan P. *Compassionate Ministry: Theological Foundations.* Maryknoll, NY: Orbis Books, 1996.

Talbert, Charles H. *Reading Luke: A Literary and Theological Commentary on the Third Gospel.* New York: Crossroad, 1982.

Tannehill, Robert C. *Luke.* Abingdon New Testament Commentaries. Nashville: Abingdon Press, 1996.

Thielicke, Helmut. *The Waiting Father: Sermons on the Parables of Jesus.* Tr. By John W. Doberstein. New York: Harper & Brothers, 1959.

Tiede, David L. *Luke.* Augsburg Commentary on the New Testament. Minneapolis: Augsburg Publishing House, 1988.

Trench, Richard C. *Notes on the Parables of Our Lord.* Westwood, NJ: Fleming H. Revell Company, 1953.

Tutu, Desmond Mpilo. *No Future Without Forgiveness.* New York: Image Books, 1999.

Ulanov, Ann Belford. "Practicing Reconciliation: Love and Work." *Anglican Theological Review* Volume 89 (Spring 2007): 227-46.

Via, Jr., Dan. *The Parables: Their Literary and Existential Dimension.* Philadelphia: Fortress Press, 1967.

Volf, Miroslav. *Exclusion and Embrace: A Theological Exploration of Identity, Other- ness, and Reconciliation.* Nashville: Abingdon Press, 1996.

Wehrli, Eugene S. *Exploring The Parables.* Philadelphia: United Church Press, 1963.

Wenham, David. *The Parables of Jesus.* The Jesus Library. Michael Green, Series Editor. Downers Grove, IL: InterVarsity Press, 1989.

Wilcock, Michael. *The Message of Luke: The Saviour of the World.* The Bible Speaks Today. Leicester: InterVarsity Press, 1979.

Wiesenthal, Simon. *The Sunflower: On the Possibilities and Limits of Forgiveness.* Revised and Expanded Edition. New York: Schocken Books, 1969.

Williams, Rowan. *Christ on Trial: How the Gospel Unsettles Our Judgement.* Grand Rapids: William B. Eerdmans Publishing Company, 2000.

———. *The Truce of God.* Grand Rapids: William B. Eerdmans Publishing Company, 2005.

Wright, N. T. *The Challenge of Jesus: Rediscovering Who Jesus Was and Is.* Downers Grove, IL: InterVarsity Press, 1999.

———. *Jesus and the Victory of God.* Christian Origins and the Question of God, Volume Two. Minneapolis: Fortress Press, 1996.

———. *Luke for Everyone.* Second Edition. London and Louisville: SPCK and Westminster John Knox Press, 2004.

Zahl, Paul F. M. *Grace In Practice: A Theology of Everyday Life.* Grand Rapids: William B. Eerdmans Publishing Company, 2007.

Index of Names

About the Author

Joel W. Huffstetler is Rector of St. Luke's Episcopal Church in Cleveland, Tennessee. Previously he served as Rector of St. Andrew's Episcopal Church in Canton, North Carolina, and as Assistant to the Rector of St. Paul's Episcopal Church in Chattanooga, Tennessee. He is a graduate (*summa cum laude*) of Elon College, and of The School of Theology, The University of the South (Sewanee), earning his Master of Divinity degree in 1990, and Doctor of Ministry degree in 2006. He also studied at Candler School of Theology, Emory University. He is the author of *Finding Our Unity in the Scriptures: Reconciliation in the Anglican Communion*, and *Pilgrimage Towards Healing and Reconciliation: A Windsor Report Study Guide*, as well as numerous articles and reviews. He and his wife Debbie live in Cleveland, Tennessee.